Beyond the
Worship Wars

Building Vital
and Faithful Worship

Thomas G. Long

The Alban Institute

Library of Congress Card Number 00-111200
ISBN 1-56699-240-0

12 11 10 09 08 07 06   W P   6 7 8 9 10 11 12 13 14

For Belle Smith Long

and

Belle Frazier Long

"Lord, you have been our dwelling place in all generations."

Psalm 90:1

Contents

On a Mother's Day many years ago, my brother and I decided to celebrate the occasion by surprising our parents with breakfast in bed. We were just kids, thoroughly inexperienced in the cooking arts, but how hard could it be to scramble eggs, fry bacon, and crack open a can of ready-made biscuits?

We knocked on their bedroom door and entered with two glasses of orange juice, a freshly picked rose, the Sunday paper, and a cheery greeting: "Happy Mother's Day!" We told them just to stay in bed, relax, and read the paper. Breakfast was on the way. They played along amiably with the game, remaining serenely in bed thumbing through the paper and ignoring the sounds from the kitchen of glass shattering and grease fires being extinguished.

In due course my brother and I marched triumphantly into their room bearing steaming plates of ten-minute eggs, carbonized bacon, and biscuits that would challenge an apprentice stonemason. It was, our parents said as they wolfed it down, the most delicious breakfast they had ever eaten. Love, evidently, is a wonderful spice.

During the course of writing this book I have often remembered that long-ago breakfast. This book is about excellence in worship and about model congregations that have achieved a high level of excitement, energy, and meaning in worship. We can learn much from these congregations about the renewal of worship and how to plan for and engage in worship well. However, we need to remind ourselves that even when Christian worship is at its best, it is much like that Mother's Day breakfast. It is always the work of amateurs, people who do this for love, kids in the kitchen overcooking the prayers, half-baking the sermons, and crashing and stumbling through the responses on the way to an act of adoration.

Essayist Annie Dillard also likens worshipers to children, but she uses a more danger-tinged image. We are, she says, "children playing on the floor with their chemistry sets, mixing up a batch of TNT to kill a Sunday morning."[1] She is right, of course. We worshipers are often oblivious to the fact that we have come close to the edge of a great abyss. "We seek your presence, O God," we pray with hardly a thought of what we are saying, forgetting that the One whose presence we so casually invoke summons the creation out of nothing, commands the moon and the stars to sing, shatters kingdoms and brings tyrants to their knees, shakes the foundations of the world, and causes the earth to melt at a single word. "Come no closer!" God told Moses. "Remove the sandals from your feet, for the place on which you are standing is holy ground" (Exod. 3:5), but we waltz into the sanctuary, babbling of golf and groceries, mindless of place. "Ushers," writes Dillard, "should issue life preservers and signal flares; they should lash us to our pews. For the sleeping god may wake someday and take offense."[2]

Episcopal priest Fleming Rutledge agrees. In one of her superb sermons, she says,

> Earlier generations spoke much more freely of 'the fear of the Lord' than we do. They understood in a way that is almost inaccessible for us that the Lord is compassionate and frightening, threatening and gracious at the same time....Only a God of fearful power is strong enough to overcome evil. It is such a God that the Bible proclaims to us. In the Old Testament, appearances of God always cause fear. That is why the angels are always saying, "Fear not."[3]

But the angels *do* say, "Fear not." Indeed, according to Matthew's gospel, the very first words the angel speaks to human beings after the resurrection are, "Do not be afraid" (Matt. 28:5). One could hardly find a better summary of the Gospel than those words: Do not be afraid. Do not be afraid—not because God lacks fearsome power, but rather because the God of all power and might has chosen *for* us and not *against* us. Fear not, because the God above all time and space has chosen to enter our time and our space and, like the father of the prodigal son, to race down the road toward us wayward children and to welcome us home with the ring and the robe and the sandals and the banquet of joy. "We are," said Paul, "children of God" (Rom. 8:16-17). Fear not.

So we enter the sanctuary like children filled with adoration, carrying our ineptly cooked but lovingly prepared liturgical breakfast. On the menu are prayers of which we know not the depth, sermons barely finished, hymns haltingly sung, the Word clumsily spoken. And there is God, like a parent patiently waiting to receive with relish and grace and kindness the burnt offerings we bring.

When Jimmy Carter was running for president of the United States, he continued to worship almost every Sunday morning in the little Baptist church in his hometown of Plains, Georgia. One Sunday as he emerged from church, a covey of reporters was waiting for him on the front lawn. They shouted the usual political questions at him, but then one of the reporters, suddenly aware of the setting, asked Carter an extraordinary thing: "If you were president," the reporter said, "and you felt that the law of the United States on some issue was in conflict with the law of God, which one would you obey?"

Carter stood there silently for a moment, blinking in the Georgia sunlight while the cameras quietly whirred and the reporters, pens poised against notepads, waited with mounting anticipation. "God's law," he announced at last. "I'd obey God's law."

Politically, it was a foolish thing to say. The president is sworn to uphold and to defend the laws of the land, and Carter had just announced to the press corps that whatever had happened to him in that little Baptist church ultimately claimed more of his loyalty than the U.S. Constitution. Potential commanders-in-chief are not supposed to say such things, and his political handlers must have inwardly groaned, wondering if their candidate had taken temporary leave of his senses.

In a way, Carter *had* taken leave of his senses. He had not lost his mind, but there in a simple clapboard sanctuary on a Sunday morning in Plains his senses had been transcended and his mind had been taken to a new and wonderful place. He had been at worship, and as hymn writer Charles Wesley phrased it, he had been "lost in wonder, love, and praise."[4] Or as old John put it in the Book of Revelation, he was "in the Spirit on the Lord's Day" (Rev. 1:10). Having just been an adoring child at home in the house of God, he was clear about where his devotion and loyalty ultimately lay.

There will be much discussion in this book about the details of worship services. We will think about music and drama, bulletins and announcements, architecture and choreography, words and symbols, planners and leaders. Important as these matters are, we should think of them as mere "kitchen details." The moment of truth in worship is when we emerge from the smoke- and grease-filled kitchen with our little trays and enter with adoration into the presence of God. There we will find that God transforms our meager loaves and fishes into a feast of joy and welcomes us as children truly at home. Then, anxious and troubled though our lives may be, we take leave of our earthbound senses. Confident that we, so often lost in the bewilderments of life, have been found at last by the One to whom we finally belong, we become lost again, this time "lost in wonder, love, and praise."

ACKNOWLEDGMENTS

The research and writing of this book were made possible by a grant from Lilly Endowment Inc., which was administered by the Alban Institute in Bethesda, Maryland, an ecumenical, interfaith organization that supports the life and work of religious congregations. Not only am I deeply grateful for this grant from Lilly and for Alban's confidence in my work; I am also particularly indebted to several people at Alban who have been of great support along the way. Alban President James P. Wind is a good friend and has been a valuable theological conversation partner in this project. Ian Evison, the director of research and resources development, provided welcome guidance in the field research and gentle prodding to get on with it. The Alban senior consultants—Terry E. Foland, Speed B. Leas, Alice Mann, Roy M. Oswald, Gilbert R. Rendle, and Edward A. White—gave superb advice at several checkpoints along the way, and managing editor David Lott has been most encouraging as the book has moved along the path to publication.

Beth Ann Gaede has served ably and patiently as my editor. She is an experienced prose rancher and an expert in spotting wayward words, wandering adjectives, maverick turns of phrase, and broken fence rails in the argument. Where you find faulty thinking or bad sentence construction, attribute that to authorial stubbornness and know that somewhere along the line Beth said, "I told you so."

Amy S. Vaughn, my research assistant, was a wonderful help to me, especially in doing thorough bibliographic research.

Most of all, though, I want to thank the churches described in this book, collectively known here as the "vital and faithful congregations." I have chosen not to provide their names and locations (though readers may recognize some of them) because all are living, growing, serving, changing congregations and not worship laboratories. I learned much from them about how worship can remain true to the trajectory of authentically Christian witness while responding boldly and creatively to the changing currents of our time. Valuable as these insights were, however, they pale beside the moving and joyful experiences of joining with these congregations in worship. Long after the ideas in this book are forgotten, I will still remember the thrill of gathering with these faithful people in praise and thanksgiving.

CHAPTER 1

Worship Wars:
A Report from the Front Lines

Recently, I attended a meeting in a downtown church in a large city. This was an "Old First Church" sort of place, a massive stone neo-Gothic building with impressive arches and beautiful stained glass windows, the kind of church that breathes history and tradition. Our group met in the handsome, wood-paneled church library. With its well-stocked shelves, mahogany tables, and overstuffed chairs, our meeting room could just as well have been the library of a prestigious law firm.

During a break in the meeting, some of the participants asked if they could see the rest of the church, so the senior pastor obligingly took us on a tour. When we entered the sanctuary, we saw what we expected to find in such a building: a vaulted ceiling, rank upon rank of carved pews, a soaring pulpit, a majestic pipe organ, a massive marble altar. But we also saw something we did not quite expect: a gleaming red drum set, complete with cymbals and snares, was placed right in the middle of the chancel. There among the medieval trappings, it looked as if it had been left by time travelers from the future. The senior pastor caught us staring at it. "Oh yes," he sniffed, rolling his eyes. "Our new youth minister likes *contemporary* worship."

One could hardly find a better image for the tensions and shifts in Christian worship today than the flashy red drums in the gray Gothic sanctuary. Christian worship in America at the turn of the 21st century is in a restless mood. In many congregations, worship has already undergone a sea change, and almost everything has a new look and a fresh sound—the music, the language, the mood, the style of sermons, the physical space, the days and times of the services, the leadership, even the clothing that worshipers wear. For some congregations, these changes in worship are just part of a more comprehensive redefinition of what it means to be a church in relationship to the culture, a pattern of change so sweeping that people are beginning to speak of them as "new paradigm" churches.[1]

Even in the more traditional "old paradigm" congregations, where the pace of change is typically slower and more cautious, there is a growing sense that we cannot do business as usual anymore and that worship styles must adjust to new cultural realities. Churches that a decade ago would never have tampered with their services are now freely experimenting with music, visuals, and drama. "For the prayers of the people this morning," intoned one worship leader, "please give your attention to the PowerPoint presentation on the screen," and no one in the congregation did a double take or seemed shocked by this high-tech insertion into the ancient rite. Figuratively, the red drum sets have been creeping steadily into the most staid of sanctuaries, and rare is the congregation that can look back over the past 20 years, or even the last decade, and not realize that its worship landscape has been significantly altered.

HIPPOLYTUS VERSUS WILLOW CREEK

Rare also is the congregation that has not felt some stress, some measure of conflict, over all this ferment in worship. No real change comes easily, but changes are especially explosive when they have to do with congregational worship. Worship lies close to the heart, and even a seemingly minor tweak in the order of worship, not to mention a radical shift in style, can set off major congregational fibrillations. Indeed, the pressure to engage in newer forms of worship has generated tension, at least to some degree, in virtually every congregation in America. Often this tension simply hangs in the atmosphere, an uneasy jostling of rival desires. Some people in the congregation wish that worship were more immediately relevant, more exciting, more dramatic, more casual, louder, more spontaneous, and more fun, while others wish it were quieter, more reverent, more traditional, more ordered, and more dignified—and no one is completely satisfied. In other churches, what is now being called "worship warfare" (one of the theaters of the broader culture wars) has broken out, with the usual round of casualties that serious church conflict generates. In still other congregations there is an uneasy balkanized truce—"You contemporary folk can have the 9 A.M. service, and you traditional people can have the 11 A.M."

There is even tension over how to describe the tension. "Traditional worship versus contemporary worship" is the most frequent formulation.

However, some critics object to these terms, arguing that pitting traditional versus contemporary implies that traditional worship is obsolete and irrelevant. *All* worship done with meaning is "contemporary," they respond. A sanctuary is not a museum, and a classic 16-century prayer prayed with conviction is just as "contemporary" as a hot-off-the-press prayer in trendy jargon, maybe more so.

Some other critics, coming at this conflict from the other direction, don't like the "traditional versus contemporary" lingo either, because it swings the bias toward "traditional" forms, implying that they represent the stable, weighty, and unchanging wisdom of the ages while "contemporary" forms are whims of the moment. Worship is always in a state of flux, they argue, ever changing, and the only tradition we really have in worship is movement and adaptation. So, when people talk about "traditional" worship, they are really just pointing to some privileged moment in the past, some snapshot of the innovations of a previous generation. People say they want to sing the "old hymns," but they do not mean Gregorian chant; they mean the 19th-century hymns like "Blessed Assurance" and "What a Friend We Have in Jesus." They say they want the traditions that have always stood in worship, but there are very few such traditions, and what people mean by "traditional" is only that which was in vogue when they were children.

And so it goes.

However we choose to describe these current tensions in congregational worship, there is an important history behind them, and we cannot comprehend the "worship wars," much less find a path to peace, until we understand how we got onto the battlefield to begin with. Much of the confusion, uncertainty, and conflict over worship today is generated by the collision of two powerful forces—forces that have developed gradually in the American church over the past 50 years and that are now engaged in a struggle over the soul of the church's worship. These forces are complex and multilayered, but for the sake of simplicity and for reasons I hope will become clear later, I am going to call them the "Hippolytus force" and the "Willow Creek force."

The Hippolytus Force

On December 4, 1963, a worship earthquake of major seismic proportion hit the Roman Catholic Church. On that day the *Constitution on the*

Sacred Liturgy, one of the most significant of the documents coming out of the Second Vatican Council, was issued, sounding the trumpet for a worship revolution. The *Constitution* called for sweeping reforms in worship, and the results were breathtaking—and controversial. Roman Catholic congregations began worshiping in their own languages (instead of Latin), and they discovered a more joyful celebration of the sacraments, a renewed emphasis on the centrality of Scripture in worship, an enlivened practice of biblical preaching, and a more active congregational participation in worship.[2]

Some Protestants watched these changes from the sidelines and felt smugly justified, thinking to themselves, "Well, it's about time the Catholics caught up with the Reformation." Keener observers, however, realized that the changes of Vatican II were far more radical than a simple imitation of the Reformation. Vatican II, to a large extent, cut through the old arguments and disputes of the Reformation and sought to penetrate to the core and essence of Christian worship. The reforms of Vatican II were seeking to produce worship that was genuinely biblical, centered in Christ, and fully congregational, worship that truly freed the whole congregation to worship as God's people.

As such, this worship earthquake in the Roman Catholic world set off massive aftershocks among Protestants. The Catholic reforms challenged Protestants to a fundamental rethinking of their own worship as well, and within a decade of the appearance of the *Constitution on the Sacred Liturgy* most of the "mainline" denominations in North America had become participants in exciting ecumenical discussions about worship and had developed dramatically fresh worship resources. United Methodists, Lutherans, Episcopalians, Presbyterians, and others all created new worship books, and one of the most remarkable characteristics of these resources is how similar they are to each other—and also to the post-Vatican II Roman Catholic services. What was happening in the wake of Vatican II was the forging of an ecumenical consensus—or at least a convergence—about worship. The churches were rediscovering the common Christian heritage in worship.

This rediscovery was accomplished in part through a recovery of the prayers and rites of the ancient church. One telling example: many of the new worship books contain eucharistic prayers (prayers of thanksgiving prayed at the Lord's Supper) that were modeled after a prayer found in the writings of Bishop Hippolytus, a third-century theologian and church leader in Rome. Why Hippolytus? Why would contemporary prayers be patterned after one over 1700 years old? Because Hippolytus' prayer is perhaps the earliest complete eucharistic prayer we possess. It comes from the headwaters of the Christian movement, from a time before the church divided east and west, Protestant and Catholic. Hippolytus' prayer symbolizes Christian worship when the church was still one, the pattern of prayer all Christians hold in common, prayer from a time before the schisms and bitter fights that were to follow.

For this reason I call this first force on the worship scene today "the Hippolytus force." It reflects a recovery movement in worship, an exhilarating rediscovery of the worship treasures that belong to the whole church. The official worship books of many denominations are shaped by "the Hippolytus force," and a good number of clergy today have been trained in this form of worship and have come to love and respect it. They know the importance of the unity of word and table, the vital connection between preaching and the sacraments, the compelling logic of the classical structure of the Lord's Day service, the value of the church's lectionary (an ecumenical list of Scripture passages to be used in worship, following the Christian year), the power of gestures such as anointing with oil in the service of baptism, the beauty of chanting the psalms, the rich tapestry of time-tested language in worship, and the jewels to be found among the great hymns of the church. In the Book of Revelation, there is a picture of the heavenly hosts at worship, singing in one voice, "Holy, holy, holy." The Hippolytus force represents the hope that all Christians everywhere may be joined in that song.

The Willow Creek Force

Ironically, just as the flood tides from Vatican II were rising and the ecumenical movement was reaching a high-water mark, another cultural tidal surge was passing over the American churches, this time from late 20th-century culture, creating a riptide effect. To put it bluntly, right at the point that the old established churches were recovering their rich common worship heritage, the culture seemed to be busily, vigorously, and thoroughly rejecting both them and their worship.

The mainline churches, which in the 1950s had been full and humming on all cylinders, began in the 1960s to sputter and to lose membership.

At first only a trickle of folk left the church, but the trickle became a stream, the stream became a river, the river a flood, and by the turn of the 21st century, millions and millions of people had vanished from the pews of the established churches. Most of these people did not go away mad; they just went away, for reasons that are still somewhat mysterious and hotly debated. Some of them migrated to independent churches, but most of them simply dropped out of church altogether.

As a result, many once-flourishing congregations grew smaller, older, and discouraged about the future. Moreover, even those church members who stayed have reported widespread boredom and disenchantment. Not everyone felt this way, of course, and not every congregation experienced decline, but the face of the American church was clearly troubled. After generations of saying yes to the church, many people in American society were now apparently saying no.

As a response to this crisis, a few visionary church leaders began to theorize that people were leaving churches not because they were tired of spirituality but because they were tired of the typical churchy kind of spirituality, tired of the boring, remote, and highly institutionalized forms in which the established churches always seemed to package the search for God. The world has changed, they argued, and people out there in the culture no longer see themselves as churchy folk trying to choose between the local Methodist and Lutheran parishes. They are, rather, "seekers," religious free agents, people untethered from conventional church loyalties, human beings hungrily searching in their own ways for spiritual experiences in very personal, immediate, often unconventional, and practical ways.

What happens, ask these leaders, when "Harry and Mary Seeker"[3] stumble, by choice or chance, into the local mainline church? Alas, they encounter "the Hippolytus force." They find (to push the point a bit) a service of worship so packed with ancient religious terminology and mystifying gestures that it may as well be the Latin Mass for all they understand of it; a repertoire of hymns they don't know and don't particularly like; dull sermons on the Bible, which they don't read anyway and don't know much about, on themes that seem abstract and irrelevant; classical music, which they despise, played on an organ, an instrument they don't enjoy; and all of this carried out by a group of seemingly dispirited, mainly elderly people who are often cold to visitors and who seem a bit bored by the whole thing themselves. In short, Harry and Mary won't be back.

What was needed, these visionaries maintained, was not a Band-Aid placed over the wound of rejection but major surgery on the life of the church, something on the scale of the Reformation—an entirely new kind of church with an entirely new way of connecting with people and a thoroughly refashioned way of worshiping. If the church is to survive and to be faithful to its evangelistic mission, then worship will have to be designed with Harry and Mary Seeker in view. A handful of churches led the way toward developing "seeker-oriented" worship, none more publicly, famously, or symbolically than the Willow Creek Community Church in South Barrington, a northwest suburb of Chicago. The Willow Creek Church is the mentor congregation of this movement, the flagship church of the seeker worship phenomenon (thus our designation of "the Willow Creek force").

What did Willow Creek Church, and others like it, do? Realizing that most "secular" people who are willing to come to church for any reason at all do so on a Sunday morning, the Willow Creek Church decided to schedule its more standard style of worship—worship for the regulars and the faithful—in the middle of the week, and to do something quite innovative on Sunday morning. Leaders turned the Sunday morning service into a completely seeker-oriented event, a bold experiment in evangelism. "[W]e decided at the inception of Willow Creek," writes senior pastor Bill Hybels, "to prioritize Harry and Mary by giving them this prime time of Sunday mornings (we later added identical service on Saturday nights)."[4]

Willow Creek leaders studied the religious attitudes and hungers of seekers and built these seeker services around what they understood to be Harry's and Mary's needs and desires. The services are contemporary in language and music; highly visual, employing dramatic skits and multimedia presentations; choreographed and paced to the "high standards in the secular marketplace" of shows, plays, and other public ceremonies; filled with messages pertinent to the issues faced by people today, with plenty of present-day illustrations and applications, and charged with clear "Christianity 101" teaching.[5]

The Willow Creek wager paid off, at least in attendance. Thousands of people throng to Willow Creek on Sundays, and hundreds of congregations have imitated Willow Creek's example. Not only were Harry and Mary Seeker coming to these churches; many of the regular members of these congregations reported that worship had never been so lively, so meaningful. The seeker-oriented style of worship turned out to have great appeal to people inside the church as well as outside, particularly young people, who responded favorably to the exciting visuals, swift pacing, and upbeat music. An astute observer of the Willow Creek scene commented that when one compares the state-of-the-art sound system and the highly polished, dramatic, and immediately relevant services at Willow Creek to the "stone church on the corner where the guy is preaching on the Hittites," the contrast is stark. "It's Wal-Mart versus the corner grocery. It ain't a fair fight."[6]

People who visited Willow Creek Church and experienced the high-energy style of service began to go back to their congregations and to lobby for some changes in worship at home. Praise bands and drama troupes and casual "blue-jeans services" sprang up all over. As the Willow Creek force took hold, worshipers flung off their neckties and straw hats and showed up in shorts and sandals and got up out of their pews and swayed to the new, hard-driving music. What began as a strategy in evangelism quickly became a movement in popular, casual, contemporary, media-inspired worship. As C. Peter Wagner, Fuller Seminary professor, has noted, a large number of churches now embody, at least in one of their services, elements of the new style:

> Worship leaders have replaced music directors. Keyboards have replaced pipe organs. Casual worship teams have replaced robed choirs. Overhead projectors have replaced hymnals. Ten to 12 minutes of congregational singing is now 30 to 49 minutes or even more. Standing during worship is the rule, although a great amount of freedom for body language prevails.[7]

So the "Hippolytus force" and the "Willow Creek force" were both at work in the life of the church, both with noble and well-grounded intentions, and they were bound to cross swords. And they have. Indeed, shock troops for the two sides have begun to hurl some nasty insults across the trenches. Some of the Hippolytus advocates tend to see the Willow Creek folk as having sold their birthright for a mess of porridge. The great worship heritage of the church, the result of centuries of carefully finding just the right patterns and words and music to praise God aright, has been thrown over for a fast-food, historically ignorant, theologically vacuous massaging of the worst consumerist impulses of our culture. Much that passes for contemporary worship is simply bad music, empty words, and superficial entertainment—in short, MTV at prayer.

The grenade-throwers on the other side charge the Hippolytus folk with antiquarianism, boring punch-the-time-clock pacing in worship, and a stubborn and selfish insistence on bells, smells, and chancel-prancing while a spiritually hungry world quietly starves to death. If the church continues to insist on worshiping in a language no one understands, with music no one can sing and services no one wants to attend, then the church will die an entirely justified death. "Father McKenzie," sang the Beatles, "writing the words of a sermon that no one will hear."

Actually, most congregations today do not find themselves firmly in either camp. Most churches are somewhere in the mixed and muddled middle, trying to sort out what their conflicts over worship mean. Clergy are often uncertain of what to do; musicians wonder how far to go in either direction. The red drums are in the gray chancel, which means that, on the one hand, a praise song or two may be woven into the regular service, or a Saturday night "contemporary service" established as an experiment, or people encouraged to dress casually for worship, and more laughter and applause heard in the sanctuary than formerly. On the other hand, the Lord's Supper may well be celebrated with more ceremony and reverence than it once was, using an ecumenical liturgy with portions of the prayers sung by the congregation, or the service of baptism may include the ancient ecumenical formula for renouncing evil. In other words, both Hippolytus and Willow Creek forces are at work simultaneously in most congregations, and the permutations that result are seemingly infinite.

FINDING A "THIRD WAY"

This book started with a conviction and a hunch. The conviction is that both the Hippolytus and Willow Creek forces, for all they have to teach us, are finally not up to the challenge of the day. In their pure forms, they both miss the mark. The Willow Creek approach (and here I speak less of the Willow Creek congregation per se and more of the whole movement toward seeker-friendly, contemporary worship) puts too much distance between itself and the Christ-centered, historically informed, theologically shaped worship that constitutes the great tradition of Christian prayer and praise that is obedient to the Gospel. It turns out in the end to be a pretty shallow pool in which to learn how to swim with maturity as a Christian.

For all the protestations that seeker-friendly worship is simply an evangelistic prelude to "real" worship, the fact is that its participants do not often view it this way. Seeker-friendly services happen on Sunday and they feature religious songs and a preacher doing something like preaching: It walks like a duck and it talks like a duck, so it must be church. Indeed, the seeker-type churches have lately faced up to the fact that getting people to make the transfer from seeker worship to "believer worship" has been more difficult than originally thought.[8]

More telling, however, is the fact that much seeker-style worship constantly betrays its roots not in the Gospel story but in the television-shaped consciousness of our time. A service of worship is a ritual, and all significant rituals spring from powerful life-changing origins. Indeed, part of the function of rituals is to allow the participants to experience vicariously that original force and to tap some of its energy anew.

A classically shaped Christian worship service is formed by the biblical story; it is in essence a recapitulation of the sacred narrative of God's interactions with human beings. When the prayer of confession is prayed, Isaiah says once again, "Woe is me, for I am one of unclean lips." When the Bible is opened, the faithful are once again at Sinai, once again at the Mount of Revelation. When a new convert steps into the waters of baptism, the people of God cross the Red Sea once again, Jesus is baptized in the Jordan once more. When the bread is broken and the wine is poured in the Lord's Supper, the congregation is there in the Upper Room, there at the cross, "for as often as you eat this bread and drink this cup, you show forth the Lord's death." To go through the order of worship is symbolically to walk through the whole narrative of faith. The service is a metaphor constantly pointing to its referent.

When the chancel is a stage, however, and the music is performed by musicians gripping hand-held mikes, and the interspersing of talk and music and skit moves with the rapid and seamless pacing of "Saturday Night Live" then the referent here is unmistakable, too. This is not a retelling of the biblical narrative; it's the recapitulation of prime time. Even if the music is stimulating, the prayers uplifting, the messages inspiring, and the experience heartwarming, the underlying structure of the service is still basically telling the wrong story, the story that will not finally take one to Christian depth but only to "see you next week, same time, same station."

On the other hand, the Hippolytus approach, unlike the Willow Creek approach, has often not taken sufficient account of the fact that we are in a new and challenging cultural environment and that worship must always be ready to adapt. The advocates of the Hippolytus force are fully aware that Christian worship is a private event. It is not a picnic softball game or a holiday parade performed for and by all comers; it is the ritual of the community of faith, of those who belong to Christ. As such, it demands a special vocabulary, a practiced set of skills, and growing knowledge of the biblical story and the meaning of worship itself.

The Hippolytus people know all of this. What they sometimes fail to recognize fully, however, is that although Christian worship is a private event, it is done in a public place. The doors and windows of the church are figuratively always open, and there is no authentic Christian worship without a genuine welcome and hospitality to the stranger. Out there in American society are millions of people who are spiritually hungry, people who have either never looked to the church as a resource or who have tried it and found it wanting. Some people have never heard what the church has to say. Others have heard it, but their memories have grown dim. If the "stranger" in our day includes the hungry spiritual seekers out there in the world who cannot find their way into our worship because the doors are locked or the language is too cryptic or the hospitality too stingy or the family rituals impossible to learn, then Christ, too, will have a difficult time getting in. "Whoever welcomes one such child in my name," Jesus said, "welcomes me" (Matt. 18:5).

Moreover, the Hippolytus style of worship, as actually practiced in local churches, is, frankly, often quite boring. It can plod along its once majestic path from gathering to blessing without much spirit, verve, or life. Sadly, the Sunday worship of many a traditional church has become something of a Chevy Bel Air: it starts every time and gets you safely from here to there, but the heart never races and the spine rarely tingles. "Wasn't church a lot easier when God didn't show up?" asks one of the new seeker church ministers, throwing an elbow at the traditional churches. "Then you knew what time you'd get home for Sunday dinner."[9]

That leads to the hunch on which this book is based. I had the intuition that some congregations had managed to avoid the hardened battle lines and had, by plan or providence or both, discovered a "third way" in worship between Hippolytus and Willow Creek. I had the strong feeling that many congregations had managed to remain firmly within the trajectory of historic Christian worship (the main contribution of the Hippolytus force) and yet had fashioned worship that is genuinely responsive to the present cultural environment and is accessible, attractive, and hospitable to religious seekers and questers outside the church (the main goal of the Willow Creek force).

The idea that there is a way through the worship wars, a way to combine the best features and healthiest impulses of the combatants, is certainly not original with me. Others have sought ways to join the virtues of the traditional and the contemporary in worship. Most notably, Robert Webber, professor of theology at Wheaton College and a distinguished expert on worship, has argued persuasively for "blended worship," a style that mixes traditional and contemporary, old and new, substance and relevance. If traditional worship is formal and contemporary worship is informal, then blended worship moves back and forth between these two styles. If traditional worship is word-driven and punctuated by organ music, and contemporary worship is music-driven with pianos, drums, and guitars, then blended worship has both. Blended worship has both hymnbooks and overhead projectors, printed prayers and free prayers, sermons and talk-back sessions.[10]

But in the final analysis, it was not "blended" worship that I sought. Webber has a fluid and sophisticated understanding of "blended" worship, but the bare word "blended" tends to convey the idea of a mix-and-match approach—a dash of contemporary thrown in with a measure of traditional. Too many congregations, in my view, have adopted this compromise—we'll do a traditional hymn, then we'll do a praise song. We'll have the classic structure, but we'll spice it up with skits. A little of this and a little of that, and everyone will be happy.

What I was looking for, instead, were congregations that had created a new thing in the earth—a service of worship completely attuned to the American cultural moment but also fully congruent with the great worship tradition of the Christian church; a service that attracts young people and seekers and the curious and those who are hungry for a spiritual encounter, but that does so by beckoning people to the deep and refreshing pool of the Gospel of Jesus Christ as it has been understood historically in the church.

At first, I wondered if I were in fact looking for a unicorn, a mythical beast I could conjure up in my imagination but that did not really exist. I would telephone friends and experts and other contacts, trying to describe the sort of congregation for which I was searching. Often I would be misunderstood, and people would recommend a church doing the Hippolytus thing well or a sexy church with rhythm-and-blues services or the latest hot megachurch on the outskirts of some city.

Slowly but surely, though, I began to build a list of congregations that were managing to carve out another path. The more I searched, the more churches I found that were, in fact, practicing the "third way" in worship. I narrowed my list to a group of about 20 churches, which I either attended in person or observed on videotape.

As I visited these remarkable congregations, worshiped with them, and spoke to their leadership, a coherent picture began to emerge. Although these churches were large and small, urban and suburban, Protestant and Catholic, white and ethnic minority, they shared certain characteristics and virtues. Varied as they were, they held some features in common, and these characteristics, it seemed to me, were transportable to other congregations seeking to renew their worship. To be sure, not every congregation possessed every single virtue, but each congregation embodied most of them. I decided to call these congregations "vital and faithful churches"—"vital" because they were active and growing and drawing crowds of people to their worship, "faithful" because they managed to remain true to the great worship heritage of the church as they did so.

These churches, needless to say, were not perfect. They have the same petty quarrels, the same staff problems, the same low Sundays that every church has. But they have found themselves in a good place in regard to worship, a place that can serve as a beacon to the rest of us, guiding us toward worship that attracts people in our society to an encounter with God in Christ.

Here are the characteristics of these churches. The chapters that follow will explore how these characteristics are expressed in congregational life and worship.

Vital and faithful congregations:

1. Make room, somewhere in worship, for the experience of mystery
2. Make planned and concerted efforts to show hospitality to the stranger
3. Have recovered and made visible the sense of drama inherent in Christian worship
4. Emphasize congregational music that is both excellent and eclectic in style and genre
5. Creatively adapt the space and environment of worship
6. Forge a strong connection between worship and local mission—a connection expressed in every aspect of the worship service
7. Maintain a relatively stable order of service and a significant repertoire of worship elements and responses that the congregation knows by heart
8. Move to a joyous festival experience toward the end of the worship service
9. Have strong, charismatic pastors as worship leaders

In the pages that follow, we will explore these congregations, discern how these characteristics are embodied in their worship, and how these elements can be transplanted in new topsoil in other congregations.

CHAPTER 2

Why Do People Come to Worship?
The Presence of Mystery

W hen a congregation wants to renew its worship, it seems obvious and natural to start by trying to figure out what attracts people to worship in the first place. After all, a healthy congregation draws people to worship who are not already a part of the church, draws people from the larger culture into the particular community and experience of worship, and if a church plods stubbornly along with worship that is boring and unappealing and does not meet people's needs, it seems inevitable that it will soon find its pews occupied by only a few determined loyalists. If we knew what compelled people to come, we could at least in theory shape worship in those directions.

So, why *do* people come to worship? Given the lures and distractions of a leisure culture, what motivates some people to choose worship over a round of golf, a couple of hours in the garden, or a casual morning lingering over bagels and the Sunday paper? Once upon a time church bells rang out to summon the whole village to worship, but we no longer live in that village. We live instead in a fragmented, diverse society in which a cacophony of bells clangs for our attention. Worship competes with a thousand rivals, from Blockbuster Video to soccer practice.

People come to worship for many reasons. Some come from habit, some from gratitude, some from guilt, some from loyalty. Some show up because they have a spouse who coaxes or coerces them to come; others come because they have a child who "needs to be brought up right." Some come out of deep conviction, and still others come for reasons of the heart they cannot quite name. But underneath it all, what beckons them to close their ears to the siren songs of our culture and to make their way to the Sunday worship?

In some ways, given the social setting and cultural trends that the church faces today, it is a wonder that people do still come to worship. Scholars say that congregations now operate in the context of "religious pluralism" and a "decline in institutional religious commitment," but in practical terms this means that, whether we live in a large city or a small town, our next-door neighbors may be Methodists or Muslims, freethinkers or fundamentalists, Baptists or Buddhists, Adventists or atheists, New Age spiritualists or just plain nothing at all. Moreover, whatever it is they do or do not believe, an increasing number of them are content to practice their religion, if they have one, in splendid isolation, finding it unnecessary or unappealing to worship in a church building with other people. As one of the people interviewed in sociologist Robert Bellah's *Habits of the Heart* put it, "I believe I have a commitment to God which is beyond church."[1]

This is not seen as good news in church circles, of course, and there is much lamenting over the general drop in attendance and the declining participation in congregational worship. However, when we consider the strong acids that eat away at congregational life today—the surging tide of individualism, the pedal-to-the-metal consumerism, the rootlessness, the disposition to manufacture "lifestyles" out of personal preferences, the loss of confidence in creeds and religious traditions, and the tendency to pick and choose religious values as if they were being offered on a Home Shopping Channel of the soul—the wonder is not that so few come to worship anymore, but that so many still do. Worship continues to appeal to many people, and if we could learn to build on its strengths and intrinsic appeal, worship could draw many more.

THE RIGHT QUESTION?

Having asked the question, "Why do people come to worship?" we need to be careful how we look for answers. We began by saying that if we could just learn what motivates people to come to worship, we could learn how to accentuate those aspects of worship and thus make worship even more attractive. At one level, this theory is true, but at another level, asking what motivates people to come to worship may turn out to be the wrong question, even a dangerous one.

Let me jump ahead of myself a bit and lay my convictional cards on the table. First, I believe that authentic worship genuinely meets people's needs because—at the risk of sounding circular in my reasoning—people need to worship. Worshiping God is not simply a good thing to do; it is a necessary thing to do to be human. The most profound statement that can be made about us is that we need to join with others in bowing before God in worshipful acts of devotion, praise, obedience, thanksgiving, and petition. What is more, when all the clutter is cleared away from our lives, we human beings do not merely *need* to engage in corporate worship; we truly *want* to worship in communion with others. All of us know somewhere in our hearts that we are not whole without such worship, and we hunger to engage in that practice. Thus, planners of worship do not *make* worship meaningful; worship is *already* meaningful. We do not manufacture worship that addresses people's deepest needs; true worship already meets those needs. Our job, then, is to get the distortions out of the way and to plan worship that is authentic, that does not obscure, indeed that magnifies, those aspects of true worship that draw people yearning to be whole.

Second, it must be said that while authentic worship will meet people's needs and thus will be attractive to people, not everything that attracts people to the sanctuary is authentic worship. Indeed, it is easier (and thus more tempting) to create events that we *call* "worship," events that attract curious crowds of people, who are drawn not genuinely to worship God but to be entertained, flattered, given cost-free therapy, provided with short-term practical advice for living, or offered any of the countless other superficial incentives that will gather people for a while.

So if we base decisions about congregational worship on what-do-people-say-they-want-in-worship "market research," matching worship styles to current fashion, taste, and popular preference, we will distort worship beyond recognition and mangle it into something alien: simply a mirror of the culture's current fancy. Whim and superficial attraction can easily be confused with more profound hungers and needs, and it is tempting to spot churches with jammed parking lots and packed seats and to assume that they have somehow discovered the secret formula. Thus, what appears to beckon people to worship are services with high-tech audiovisuals and video-game pacing or those with humor-laced skits on "real life" issues like handling pressure and family conflict or those with no-compromise sermons on tough Bible truths or those with high-energy folk-rock bands pumping out "Shine, Jesus, Shine," or whatever else operates as the popular liturgy *du jour* in our community.

It is important to keep reminding ourselves of the strange truth that, odd as it may sound, worship is best measured not by how popular, inspirational, beautiful, educational, musically rich, poetic, or exciting it is. Good worship often is all of these things, indeed true worship has its own beauty, takes dramatic shape, summons the best of language, music, and the arts, and powerfully lifts the human heart. But if we make any of these qualities the goal or primary standard of worship, we have badly missed the point. In essence, worship is what happens when people become aware that they are in the presence of the living God. Trying to turn worship into something useful outside this encounter or attempting to make it cosmetically more appealing misunderstands its basic character. Worship is and should be, to borrow theologian and worship scholar Marva Dawn's evocative phrase, "a royal waste of time."[2]

In this way, worship is a lot like falling in love. When someone falls heads over heels for another, adoration flows naturally from the lover toward the loved one. This adoration is not primarily about anything else, nor does it serve any utilitarian purpose outside the love relationship. Indeed, in the presence of the loved one, the lover cannot help but adore, and apart from the beloved, nothing can provoke adoration—not perfume or soft music or dim lights or wine and roses.

Just so, at the heart of worship is an encounter with the living God, and true worship involves human beings falling down before God's presence. Worship is about awe, not strategy. If we are trying to find ways to "get" people to church, maybe we can succeed in enticing them, but if we are trying to find ways to "get" people truly to worship, we cannot. The burning bush was not choreographed to appeal to Moses' instincts for worship, it was the manifestation of God's presence before which Moses could only flee or bow down. When Jesus walked across a storm-tossed sea to his disciples, as they struggled to keep their boat from being swamped by the staggering waves, they worshiped him (Matt. 14:33). They did so not because the experience was entertaining, educational, or aesthetically pleasing but because it involved an overwhelming experience of the Other. In worship, human beings respond to the God who is already there, and our worship is the fullness of what pours out of us when we become aware of God's presence—awestruck praise, immeasurable joy, trembling confession, grateful self-giving.

Now, having said this, we can look at the other side of the coin. It is true that worship is primarily about the presence of God and not about human need, but it follows that people do need to worship because people need to be in relationship with God. In this sense, therefore, worship does meet human need and is, in a profound way, both attractive and useful. This understanding of how worship meets human need is quite different from the "market research" approach. We are not making a list of human tastes and desires and then trying to figure out how to pound the pegs of worship into those holes. Rather, we are working in the other direction, asking how authentic worship evokes from us what is genuinely human and satisfies our deepest longings.

Putting these ideas once again in bluntly practical terms, it would be possible to design worship services with glitter appeal, services that would draw a crowd (and many churches have impressively done so). Such worship would probably be high on entertainment value, would perhaps address the loneliness in our culture by helping people feel a part of a group, and would be worth the time spent because it would provide practical tools for facing the problems of daily living. But for all its attractiveness, such an event would not be true worship, not only because our needs for entertainment, intimacy, and self-help can be met as well or better in other places, but also because these are not, when all is said and done, our very deepest needs.

What are our deepest needs? First and foremost, we need mystery, that is, we need God. Specifically, we need to be in communion with God, to belong to God, to be in right and loving relationship with God. The 16th-century Heidelberg Catechism points to this need to belong to God when it begins with the following question and answer: "What is your only comfort, in life and in death? That I belong—body and soul, in life and in death—not to myself but to my faithful Savior, Jesus Christ."[3]

Second, because we belong to God, we need to join ourselves in community with others to give ourselves away to God, to offer our lives to something larger than ourselves, something that provides meaning and lets us know that our lives count for something of ultimate value. Underneath all the narcissism and selfishness of our time lies a deeper human hunger to be a part of a larger whole, to give ourselves away to a great cause, to join with others in pouring out our lives for something that genuinely matters. Philosopher and anthropologist Ernst Becker concludes his monumental work *The Denial of Death* by stating, "The most that any one of us can seem to do is to fashion something—an object or ourselves—and drop it into the confusion, make an offering of it, so to speak, to the life force."[4] Extending Becker's insight in a more theological direction, what people need is to offer themselves—their energies, their work, their play, their relationships, everything—to God. In other words, what truly gives life meaning is not the acquisition of things for ourselves but, to the contrary, giving ourselves away, self-offering, human beings profoundly desire to enter life's great sanctuary and symbolically to place themselves on the altar. As the old hymn puts it, "Take my life, and let it be consecrated, Lord, to thee."

When these two needs are met in worship—mystery and communal meaning—worship becomes a refreshing pool toward which people are drawn. When these needs are not met, worship betrays its true self and, to persuade people to show up and to remain, frantically begins to steal energy, content, and style from other sources, like television, pop psychology or the self-help movement.

In the next chapter, we will examine the connection between worship and the second need, the need for communal meaning. The remainder of this chapter will delve into the theme of mystery and will explore the first characteristic of worship in vital congregations.

> **CHARACTERISTIC 1.**
> VITAL CONGREGATIONS MAKE ROOM,
> SOMEWHERE IN WORSHIP,
> FOR THE EXPERIENCE OF MYSTERY.

IN THE PRESENCE OF MYSTERY

Barbara Brown Taylor, who is well known as a fine preacher and writer, is an Episcopal priest who spent part of her ministry as a coordinator of Christian education in a local parish. She reports that she periodically surveyed her congregation to inquire about what sort of adult church-school classes they desired. The answer was predictable and unwavering: more courses on the Bible. Every quarter, they clamored for more Bible. Curiously, though, when she arranged for professors from a nearby seminary to teach classes on the Bible, attendance was poor. Quarter after quarter, it was Bible study the members of the congregation said they wanted, but no one came to the classes. "Finally," she notes, "I got the message. 'Bible' was a code word for 'God.' People were not hungry for information about the Bible; they were hungry for an experience of God, which the Bible seemed to offer them."[5]

In like manner, people are not hungry for more worship services, for more hymns, sermons, and anthems. They are hungry for experiences of God, which can come through worship; in the most primal sense, this hunger is what beckons people to worship. The anticipation of the holy is almost palpable, even in the tiniest church on the most routine of days. One can feel it as the people gather, in the spaces between the prayers and hymns, in the almost electric silence before the homily. Novelist and essayist Frederick Buechner captures this sense of expectation in a moving passage in his book *Telling the Truth.* He pictures a Sunday preacher entering the pulpit, switching on the lectern light, and spreading out his sermon notes "like a poker hand." Buechner goes on to say:

> All of this deepens the silence with which they sit there waiting for him to work a miracle, and the miracle they are waiting for is that he will not just say that God is present, because they have heard it said before . . . but that he will somehow make it real to them. They wait for him to make God real to them through the sacrament of words.[6]

Now obviously, an encounter with God is not something that human beings control or arrange. No worship planning team could or should sit around a table brainstorming ways for holiness to erupt in the order of worship. However, while we certainly do not have the power to make God appear, a service of worship is a somewhat fragile medium, and we do have, it seems, the negative capacity to create static, to sabotage people's perception of God's presence. God is present in worship; our job is to clear the clutter and get out of the way of people's sight lines.

One Sunday morning, I happened to be at worship in a small, informal suburban church, arriving a few minutes before the service started. The worship space was simple but reverent—a spray of flowers on a stand at the front, an open Bible on the communion table, a prominent baptismal font and pulpit. The organist was playing a quiet prelude as the ushers handed out bulletins and guided people with dignified hospitality to their pews. As the music continued, a door at the front of the sanctuary opened, and through it the choir and minister entered and moved in procession to their places. In short, it was like a hundred thousand other churches on a hundred thousand other Sundays in a hundred thousand other neighborhoods. There was nothing extraordinary about the congregation, the furnishings, the ushers, the music, or the opening sequence of events. Nevertheless, there was, in the gathering of the congregation and the entrance of the worship leaders, a growing feeling of expectation, a mounting sense of drama, a mood in the room that something significant and full of mystery was about to happen.

Then, abruptly, a worshiper seemed to catch the minister's eye, and a look crossed the minister's face that said, "I just remembered something I forgot to tell you." The minister got up, and as the puzzled congregation followed his trajectory, he ambled down the center aisle, leaned over the end of the pew where the person was sitting, and the two exchanged a few words. Then the pastor returned to the chancel, blithely unaware that his action—no doubt innocent and well intentioned—had nonetheless damaged worship by breaking the mood of expectation and disrupting the dramatic flow so essential to the perception of mystery. In how many ways, small and large, do worship leaders perform similar acts of liturgical vandalism, subverting the capacity of worship to serve as a meeting place with God?

Much about maintaining a sense of awe and mystery in worship depends, it seems, upon what is sometimes called "presidential style," a somewhat clumsy technical term used to describe the way leaders act in worship. Sometimes "presidential style" is treated as if it were purely a matter of acquired technique, but it actually flows more from conviction. If the leaders genuinely believe that worship is being conducted in the presence of God, it shows, and what is more, that belief is contagious. Whether the leaders are eloquent or prosaic, formal or informal, experienced or novice, when they perceive that worship occurs in the context of holy mystery, everything changes—voice, posture, language, gesture. Conversely, if the worship leaders are convinced that nothing is happening in the sanctuary beyond the projection of their own personalities, that shows, too, and worship becomes merely theater and is compressed to the exclusively horizontal.

To see how body, voice, and gesture are affected by context, conviction, and self-awareness, notice how people behave at a fast-food stand compared to how they function in an elegant, candle-lit restaurant. In the first, they saunter casually to the counter, rattle off their order, perhaps turning to shout to a friend at a table in the eating area, "What d'ya want on your cheeseburger?" When people go to a fine restaurant, however, they enter with a certain cautious dignity. They speak to the maître d' softly and carefully, and they stay alert to the ceremonies and rituals of formal dining.

Just so, presiders at worship who have a sense of place, who remain aware that worship occurs in the presence of the holy, carry themselves accordingly. Their bodies and voices convey a sense of place, and they respond to the interior rhythms and realities of an encounter with the holy. This does not mean, though, that they march around like wind-up clergy dolls. As liturgical scholar Robert Hovda has observed, "Reverence is not stiffness and pomposity—quite the opposite, for those qualities involve a self-assertion and a feeling of self-importance that are antithetical to reverence."[7]

In his wonderful book *Holy Things*, worship professor Gordon Lathrop raises the suggestion that a key to the experience of the holy in worship is the maintaining of a dialectic, a tension, between strangeness and welcome.[8] On the one hand, we are welcome at worship, and we are at home here. We are God's people, and the sanctuary is a place of familiarity. On the other hand, we must not become so familiar that we lose the capacity to be surprised by grace. We must not feel so at home that we lose the aware-ness that we are pilgrims and strangers traveling in a land of wonderment, not of our own making. The worship leader who can maintain this tension goes a long way toward making the service an environment for mystery.

Take, as an example of this tension between strangeness and wel-come, a common action in many services of worship: the reading of the Bible. How should the Bible be treated to convey a proper sense of mys-tery? One can imagine errors in both directions. On the one hand, some worship leaders, eager to puncture ancient superstitions, are zealous to trample down the flowerbed by treating the Bible casually, even carelessly, as if to say, "Hey, folks, relax. It's just a *book*," or more devastating, "I'm in charge here. The focal point is *me*, not this reading of Scripture." Such overfamiliarity with holy things is clumsy at best and malicious at worst. On the other hand, one can imagine a mistaken overemphasis on strangeness, a worship leader who handles the Bible like a magician's handkerchief, wav-ing it pretentiously through the air in motions of awkward and finally mean-ingless pomp. Far better is the worship leader who handles the Bible with proper familiarity—opening its pages gratefully, as a member of the com-munity who has been blessed here many times before, reading with the relish of one who knows these stories and sayings well—*and* with fitting awe, as one who recognizes the Bible as a symbol of otherness and mys-tery outside ourselves, as one who never knows what new wonder will be disclosed, as one who is prepared to be surprised by an unexpected word from beyond.

Other than reverence by the leaders, how else is mystery communicated in worship? There are many ways, from the architecture of the sanctuary to silence to the posture of prayer. Years ago, practical theologian James Dittes of Yale University argued that even the people's habit of crowding into in the rear pews of the sanctuary to avoid sitting toward the front, the subject of many jokes, may in fact express a tacit "awe of the holy."[9]

Frederick Buechner once remarked that he had learned something about perceiving the holy in life while traveling on a British freighter across the Atlantic. A red-haired junior officer had been on watch during the night, looking for the lights of other ships on the dark sea, and he told Buechner that the way to see lights on the horizon was not to look directly at the horizon but instead at the sky just above it. Just so, Buechner observed, the way to discern the holy dimension of life is not to look directly at it, but "just above it, or off to one side."[10]

So, while we cannot observe the holy with a direct gaze, we can see evidences of it with indirect glances at various aspects of worship. For some congregations, mystery makes its way in via solemn processions and grand gestures, for others through joining hands in a circle around the communion table for prayer, for still others through the play of light and shadow in the sanctuary, and for others through compelling preaching or the spontaneous singing of choruses or unhurried moments of silence. But regardless of how it comes, every church with vital worship—large or small, formal or informal—has a moment, a space when the congregation becomes aware that it is not alone but in the presence of mystery.

Thinking about how many congregations have lost any sense of the transcendent in worship, Lutheran theologian Joseph Sittler maintained, "What is needed is a concentrated attack on the lost realms of wonder and terror and ambiguity, which lie so shallowly beneath the shallow chatty, bland life of our Sunday-morning parish situation—an attack equipped for its work by biblical knowledge, theological acumen, and a shared awareness of the infinite equivocations in the lives of the people who still come, even expectantly, to our churches."

CHAPTER 3

Why Do People Come to Worship?
A Sense of Belonging

The Jewish journalist and raconteur Harry Golden, author of *Only in America*, was a popular essayist and public speaker of a generation ago. In one of his essays, he said that as a boy he was puzzled and troubled by his father's religious habits. Although his father loudly and frequently proclaimed his agnosticism, he nonetheless never missed a service at the local synagogue. Every time the doors of the house of prayer were open, Golden's father was there. When Harry became a teenager, he finally mustered up the courage to confront his father's seeming hypocrisy. "You always say you doubt that God exists," sputtered the younger Golden, "but you go to synagogue all the time anyway. Why?"

"There are many reasons why one would go to synagogue," replied his father. "Take Silverberg. He goes to talk to God. Me? I go to talk to Silverberg."

Why do people come to worship? In the last chapter, we asserted that vital and faithful worship meets two profound human needs, the need for communion with God and the need for human community, and in his own wry way, Golden's father was pointing to the second of these needs. People are drawn to worship not only to be in the presence of God but also to be in the presence of other people—people who know our names and shake our hands and welcome us into the circle. We go to worship not just "to talk to God" but also "to talk to Silverberg."

Congregations have always known this, of course. From love feasts to camp meetings to sewing circles to youth groups to women's missionary societies to men's associations to family-night suppers to the small-group movement of today, churches have found ways to bring people together and to address not only the need to commune with God but also the desire for companionship and belonging.

GOD AND COMMUNITY—RIVALS?

Recently, however, the idea has been gaining momentum that the culture is changing on this point and that these two needs—the hunger for communion with God and the hunger for human community—are competitors, or at least are seen as disconnected from each other. Do people now want God without the entanglement of community or do they thirst for community without the encumbrance of God? Social critics cannot seem to decide which way the cultural tide is actually flowing.

Weighing in on one side are some sociologists who maintain that people today are intensely interested in spirituality and are off on all manner of hot religious quests, but that they are less and less interested in joining with others to do so. In other words, they want the God side but not the community engagement side. The case for this shift toward God and away from community is made by pointing to an apparent paradox: while religion is "cool," church is "cold." On the one hand, there are many indications of a high level of religious interest in society, even fervor, such as the remarkable increase in sales of books on popular religion, the rise of "new age" and Eastern religions, and the consistent way that the vast majority of people describe themselves in polls and surveys as religious and employ religious language and ideas self-referentially. On the other hand, involvement in mainline churches has declined sharply in the last 50 years. Membership is down, and attendance at worship has plummeted.[1] Put it all together, and a picture emerges of a society of lonely religious pilgrims who seek God, who are as spiritually hungry as ever but not in traditional ways and not through traditional religious communities. In short, people want to talk to God, but they are happy to do so without Silverberg.

Several years ago I visited one of the "drive-in" churches that sprang up in the Sunbelt in the late '50s and early '60s. This sanctuary of this church featured a large window overlooking a portion of the parking lot where the spaces were equipped with drive-in movie-style speakers. Worshipers had the choice of coming inside for worship or participating in the privacy of their cars, viewing the service through the window and listening over the speakers. The pastor of the church told me that he had once tried an experiment that he would never attempt again. Concerned that the worshipers who chose to remain in their cars were isolated and deprived of the full sense of corporate worship, he invited them one Sunday to get out of their cars and to "pass the peace" to each other in the parking lot.

This invitation was greeted by the sound of engines starting and the screeching of tires as almost every car sped away from the lot. So much for community.

This notion of disconnected, spiritual free agents fits, of course, into more comprehensive theories of the deterioration of institutional life and public commitment generally, and no one has presented the evidence for this concept more engagingly or provocatively than political scientist Robert Putnam, author of *Bowling Alone: The Collapse and Revival of American Community*.[2] Putnam maintains that, just as economies depend upon monetary capital, societies depend upon the glue of "social capital"—that is, the public trust, the spirit of volunteerism, the willingness to cooperate with others, and the community vision necessary to motivate people to work together for the common good. Putnam argues that virtually every indicator of social capital—such as PTA membership, mainline church membership, and labor union membership—has declined steadily for the past four decades. His somewhat playful signature example is that the number of people who bowl regularly has increased significantly in the last 40 years while the number of people who belong to bowling leagues has dramatically declined. In every area of life, then, including religion, Americans are "bowling," but they are "bowling alone."

Ironically, while sociologists are pressing the case for a society high on personalized religion and low on community engagement, some church leaders are heading in the opposite direction. If the church is to grow, they say, we must emphasize friendliness and downplay the overtly religious. They see an intimacy-hungry culture, especially among those of the baby-boom generation and younger, but a culture put off by God-talk, the distant mysteries of formal liturgy, and the churchly trappings of religion. So such leaders are deliberately designing the experience of church around these desires. As one astute observer described this move away from anything that smacks of the transcendent: "No spires. No crosses. No robes. No clerical collars. No hard pews. No kneelers. No biblical gobbledygook. No prayerly rote. No fire, no brimstone. . . . No forced solemnity. . . . Centuries of . . . Christian habit are deliberately being abandoned, clearing the way for new, contemporary forms of worship and belonging."[4]

If we want to draw people from this culture to worship, these intimacy-attuned church leaders claim, then the sign on the front lawn of the church should not read "Come in to meet the holy mystery" but "Come in to be known, welcomed, and loved." Timothy Wright, a pastor at a high-growth church in the Southwest and an authority on new forms of worship, states:

People today crave intimacy. They want to be known and loved
for who they are. They come to church in the hope that someone
will love them, that someone will accept them just as they are.
They value a warm, open environment. Worship services that pro-
mote intimacy will win them over.[4]

Wright believes that people also want to "know God" in a personal and
interior way, but the presenting need is to be related to other people. Thus,
worship that is overtly directed toward God (what Wright calls "liturgical
worship") is the enemy of this longed-for intimacy. The problem with liturgical worship, Wright insists, is that it is "God-directed rather than people-
directed," and thus "it lacks the relational and intimacy aspects that people
value today."[5] In short, people are drawn to worship mainly out of a need to
be known and to form warm relationships, and an overdose of transcendence can frighten them away. The solution, Wright says, is to "warm up"
the service by adding relational, intimacy-oriented elements, such as name
tags, easy-to-sing hymns, and "informal heart prayers."[6]

Indeed, the Willow Creek Church, as well as many of the congregations that have followed Willow Creek's lead, have developed strong small-
group ministries as a way of addressing this yearning for intimacy. "The
perfume of these groups may be Christian," comments Charles Trueheart
in *The Atlantic Monthly*, "but their integument is social."[7]

WHAT TO DO?

If the need for God and the need for community have become disconnected, then it is difficult for planners of congregational worship to know
what to do. If people are hungry for God but would just as soon engage in
their spiritual quests alone, then worship could attempt to appeal to that
desire by accenting the meditative and the mystical and minimizing the communal and institutional. Finally, though, this strategy will be done in by the
fact that congregations are inescapably *congregations*. There is no way to
escape the truth that congregations are groups of people with at least a
basic institutional structure gathered together for worship and mission. Congregational worship is not the same as private worship or interior spiritual
questing. Praying and singing together creates an awareness of the other,
and awareness of the other discloses social and ethical expectations and

demands. I cannot sit on the pew praying next to the long-time member or the first-time visitor without recognizing somewhere in my soul that we are not just praying simultaneously but that we are praying together, that at some level we belong to each other and are accountable to and responsible for each other.

On the other hand, if people are seeking companionship with other people but are put off by "God-directed" worship and formal talk of God, then the church could develop a strategy of easing people gradually into full worship. Services designed for the seekers of intimacy could be designed. First-name friendliness could be emphasized, and visitors could be welcomed warmly and incorporated quickly into small groups. The transcendent and vertical dimensions of worship could be muted in favor of the horizontal. God-talk and theological vocabulary could be transformed into more immediately life-relevant messages, and religious commitments could be postponed until this more urgent need for intimacy is met.

This approach has, of course, already been adopted by the hundreds of congregations sometimes called "seeker-driven" churches, the sorts of churches we described in chapter 1 under the banner "the Willow Creek force." However, we now have enough experience with this approach to have learned that these congregations often run aground in shallow water. A man in his 30s who had been a regular at a seeker-oriented megachurch made a not-untypical observation: "At first, it was amazing. I found a warmth I had never experienced growing up in the Presbyterian Church. People knew my name and made me feel so welcome. The services were enjoyable and gave me insights I could use in my real life. But after a while I started going less, then stopped altogether. I don't know why, really. It got to be 'same old, same old.' I wanted something more, something deeper."

Sally Morgenthaler's *Worship Evangelism: Inviting Unbelievers into the Presence of God*, written from a strongly evangelical perspective, recounts several cases of congregations and pastors burned out on horizontal, seeker-driven, performance-oriented worship. "The seeker event we were offering," said one pastor cited by Morgenthaler, "wasn't cutting it for some of the seekers who were coming. They were looking for something with more of a 'spiritual' feel to it."[8] She also quotes Stephen Witt, pastor of a Vineyard church, who reports: "For the past two years I have worked to make our church a 'seeker sensitive' congregation where visitors would feel welcome. . . . Visitors were assured of an abbreviated yet quality time of worship followed by a culturally relevant message. . . . [However], we hadn't adequately considered how we might also welcome the Holy Spirit."[9]

A THEOLOGICAL SOUNDING

As we think about planning for worship that is truly responsive to human need, we should step back and look theologically at the relationship between these two hungers—the hunger for God and the hunger for human community. The fact is, as we pointed out in the last chapter, that we human beings hunger for both God and community, or to put it more precisely, we hunger for God *in* community. "It is not good for humanity to be alone," states the Book of Genesis, and from the very beginning human beings were created not to be alone but to be in relationship with God and others, to encounter God in and through our companionship with others. If we listen carefully, we can hear this hunger for God in community in the cries of our culture. But we must listen very carefully indeed, with an alertness to the inner rhythms of speech, a sensitivity to the places where silence points to that which cannot be said, because people in contemporary society often lack the language and the thought categories to be able to articulate their deepest religious needs. Ideas about God, spirituality, community, and self have been downsized, and it is no wonder that people speak in small ways about large hungers. We express satisfaction over finding a friendly small group or speak joyfully about rare moments of inner spiritual illumination when we are actually pointing to our desire for a rich and full experience of encountering God in the midst of a committed community.

Sociologist Richard Sennett has argued that we live in what he calls "the intimate society,"[10] a social order developed over the last two centuries in which the individual self is the basic unit, and the values of the self are defined in private, interior, intimate, even romantic terms. It is understandable, then, that when people describe those things that matter most, they rely on the language of intimacy; it is the default-drive vocabulary of our time. Thus, when we speak today of the need for communion with God, we tend to express it in smallish, personalistic phrases such as wanting to be "more spiritually attuned," or desiring to be "centered" and to have a "spiritual self," or seeking to achieve "personal harmony with God." The language of such a quest is the vocabulary of friendship and personal relationships. We want to be "close to God," to "experience God in every moment," to "feel at one with God," to "find God within," and we want to do these things by ourselves, or at most with a few like-spirited companions.

Likewise, when we speak of the need for human community, we also use intimate terms. We want to be "accepted for who we are," we desire to be "loved" and to find a "marriage of spirits" and "mutual understanding," to be treated with "authenticity and honesty" and to be "warmly received and embraced" by others.

The central problem with the language of intimacy is that it finally cannot carry the full freight of human nature and human need. Our relationships to God and to others are broad, deep, and complex. When we narrow our descriptions of these relationships to language borrowed from the private, interior, intimate dimension of life, much that is important about these relationships slips from our grasp. More to the point, when we think about the goals of worship exclusively in intimate terms—either intimacy with God, intimacy with others, or both—the result is that worship is diminished.

For example, one book on planning contemporary worship describes the hunger to encounter God in worship this way:

> Of all the things that might motivate persons to come to our churches in the first place, it is frequently a longing for religious experience that is most predominant. . . . [T]his desire for an experiential encounter with God often plays a determining role in the religious affiliations that are chosen.
>
> . . . This experiential dimension of faith, this direct encounter with God for the individual and within the community, is at the heart of contemporary worship. Whether it be contemplative in form or profoundly expressive, the faith has to make contact, and it has to make contact on a very basic, emotional level. It is not sufficient to talk *about* a relationship with God; the relationship *must actually occur in the present moment.*[11]

Note the intimate language—"an experiential encounter with God," a "direct encounter with God," "faith on a very basic, emotional level," a "relationship with God that actually occurs in the present moment." This all seems quite wonderful until we hold it up against the full biblical witness. To be sure, there are "direct encounters with God" narrated in the Bible, but they are not all about the intimate, self-affirming values of warmth and gentleness. Some of these encounters leave human beings hiding their faces before the holy presence, trembling in awe and wonder before the *mysterium tremendum*. Also, most of the encounters with God in the Bible are not direct, face-to-face engagements at all but are mediated through prophets and priests, strangers and signs, dreams and visions, the practices of the community and the preaching of the apostles.

The Bible speaks, of course, of times when God is experienced "in the present moment," but the Bible also tells the truth about times when the face of God is hidden from human view and God's presence is not immediately felt. In the Old Testament, the hiddenness of God is one of the characteristics that separates Yahwism from the worship of Baal, the Canaanite fertility god. Baal was always present, always ready to provide powerful religious experiences. As theologian Hendrikus Berkhof observed, "Baal's presence was visible and his blessings were more or less predictable; moreover, there were magical means one could use to force these blessings in case they were long in coming. The faith in Yahweh made a poor showing compared with this fertility religion."[12] In short, if one desires an intimate encounter with the holy at every service, then go to the Temple of the Baal. Yahweh, the true and living God, sometimes withdraws from present experience. In sum, God does not always move us, and everything that moves us is not God.

What we need, then, in thinking about worship, is to sharpen our theological ears so that we can both to listen *to* the culture with respect and to listen *through* the culture with insight and deeper understanding. When we listen to the culture, we will hear a yearning for God and a yearning for human community, albeit expressed in language far too small and individualistic and full of contradictions. When we listen through the culture, we can hear people hungering for more than they know how to say, for true community and for the living God.

From Intimacy to Hospitality

As we plan for worship, then, we should replace the category of intimacy with one that is deeper theologically, namely "hospitality to the stranger." In his thoughtful book *The Company of Strangers*, Quaker educator Parker Palmer launches a critique of what he calls our culture's "ideology of intimacy," a nest of attitudes that together posit that the main purpose of human life is the development of autonomous, individual personalities and that this development takes place only within the context of warm, intimate, interior-directed relationships.[13] In *Welcoming the Stranger: A Public Theology of Worship and Evangelism*, theologian Patrick Keifert builds on Palmer's critique and provides a provocative assessment of the damage this "ideology of intimacy" can do to public worship. When congregations import private and intimate images into their worship planning, Keifert argues, the attempt to make the church a warm, friendly, family-like environment backfires. "It is precisely this projection of the private onto the public that excludes so many strangers, both inside and outside." Keifert calls upon the church in its thinking about worship to replace the theologically insufficient category of intimacy with the biblical category of "hospitality to the stranger." He states, "Hospitality to the stranger implies wisdom, love, and justice—rather than intimacy, warmth, and familiarity—in our dealings with others in public."[14]

To put this issue of hospitality to the stranger into practical terms, imagine that you are one of the greeters at the door of the church welcoming people to worship. A couple you do not recognize—visitors, strangers— come to the door. How are you to view these people and what is your responsibility toward them? Should you imagine that the most important thing you can know about these visitors is that they bring needs for intimacy that you and the congregation are to meet? Should you assume that they have come "in the hope that someone will love them, that someone will accept them just as they are, and [that] they value a warm, open environment"? To do so would be presumptuous and theologically naïve. It would assume that these visitors are really just like you, that there are no real differences between you and them, and that the highest goal possible is that you and the other members of your congregation will become intimate friends with them and invite them into the private spaces of your life.

The reality, however, is that these people are not exactly like you; indeed, they may not be much like you at all. They are the other, strangers, different. Because they are the other, they bring the promise of gifts and wisdom the congregation does not yet have. Because they are different, they also bring challenges and potential dangers. They may be hard to accept, disruptive, or even violent, or they may have needs, financial or otherwise, beyond the capacities of your congregation to meet. Regardless of their promise or their danger, the church is called to be hospitable to these strangers, and you are on the front line of this ministry. This hospitality goes far beyond the narrow bounds of modern notions of intimacy and self-fulfilling friendship. Like Abraham and Sarah by the oaks of Mamre, we are commanded to show hospitality when strangers appear at the flap of the tent, to open our house and table and God's house and table to these strangers so that they will find safe lodging, nourishment, cool water for the face, the oil of blessing, and rest for the soul.

So when you stand there in the entrance of your church, offering hospitality to these visitors, you are doing far more than simply being a nice person issuing a cheery welcome. You are showing the hospitality of God. As church historian Christine Pohl states in her fine book *Making Room: Recovering Hospitality as a Christian Tradition*, "A life of hospitality begins in worship, with a recognition of God's grace and generosity. Hospitality is not first a duty and responsibility; it is first a response of love and gratitude for God's love and welcome to us."[15]

A third-century church manual, the *Didascalia*, points to the importance of this hospitality when it faces the very practical question of what the church should do if the arrival of a stranger poses an inconvenience:

> If a destitute man or woman, either a local person or a traveler, arrives unexpectedly, especially one of older years, and there is no place, you, bishop, make such a place with all your heart, even if you yourself should sit on the ground, that you may not show favoritism among human beings, but that your ministry may be pleasing before God.[16]

What kind of institution is this? The leader, the bishop, the top person should sit on the ground if necessary to show hospitality to an old and destitute stranger? Why? What is at stake? First of all, justice is at stake. These Sunday morning visitors may look as though they are "church shopping," but the truth is, like all of us, they are on a wearying and perilous journey through life, and hospitality along the road is a matter of life and death. To greet them with generosity and welcome in the name of Christ, to make a place for them in God's house, is not just friendliness—it is a saving grace.

But even more is at stake than justice for the stranger. We show hospitality to strangers not merely because they need it, but because we need it, too. The stranger at the door is the living symbol and memory that we are all strangers here. This is not our house, our table, our food, our lodging; this is God's house and table and food and lodging. We were pilgrims and wanderers, aliens and strangers, even enemies of God, but we, too, were welcomed into this place. To show hospitality to the stranger is, as Gordon Lathrop has observed, to say, "We are beggars here together. Grace will surprise us both."[17]

Finally, there is the promise that by showing hospitality to others, we receive the very presence of God. "Whoever welcomes one such child in my name welcomes me," Jesus taught his disciples (Matt. 18:5). "Do not neglect to show hospitality to strangers," encourages the Epistle to the Hebrews, "for by doing that some have entertained angels without knowing it" (Heb. 13:2). The Egyptian monk Brother Jeremiah once said, "We always treat guests as angels—just in case."[18] As Keifert states, "[W]hen . . . biblical characters encounter the stranger face-to-face, they encounter not only another person who cannot be reduced, without remainder, to analogies of themselves, but they encounter the ultimate Stranger, the irreducible Other, God. 'Lord, we were just standing at the door of the church with a handful of worship programs. When did we see you?' 'I was a stranger, and you welcomed me.'"

Indeed, it is precisely this commitment to the stranger that forms the second characteristic of worship in vital congregations:

> ### CHARACTERISTIC 2.
> VITAL AND FAITHFUL CONGREGATIONS
> MAKE PLANNED AND CONCERTED EFFORTS TO SHOW
> HOSPITALITY TO THE STRANGER.

When the notion of hospitality to the stranger is understood theologically and freed from shallower notions of intimacy, we discover that welcoming people to worship is far more complex than simply being "a friendly church." To be sure, people need to be treated with kindness and generosity, but that is not all they need. They need to be welcomed into the house and graciously invited to the table, but that is not all they need. What do people most deeply need? Viewed theologically, people need to be welcomed into God's house, recognized and known by name, and joined with others in offering their lives to God in acts of mission. We can divide this broad need into its three constituent parts:

a. People want to be welcomed into God's house. Welcoming people into God's house is first of all a matter of architecture, and the building itself either beckons the visitor or throws up a barrier. Recently I was working with the worship committee of a congregation. The group members wanted to revitalize their church's service of worship and make the service more welcoming to visitors. As an exercise, I asked the group to walk outside the church and to imagine that they were first-time visitors. As they stood on the sidewalk looking at the church building, trying to put themselves in the shoes of a newcomer, it was clear that a visitor would spot the main door of the sanctuary and guess that this was the way in to worship. But when we walked up the steps to that door, it was locked. "This door is always locked," said a committee member. "Even on Sundays."

"Why is that?" I asked.

"None of us in the congregation use this door," he said. "We all use the side door over by the parking lot."

Many church buildings are like that one, puzzles and labyrinths whose secrets are known only to insiders. Good signage, helpful greeters, even well-designed changes in traffic patterns or, in rare cases, a rebuilding project can all make the building more a place of welcome. One of the vital congregations studied has a jazz band playing on the front steps of the church a half-hour before worship begins—a symbol that God's party is about to begin inside and that all are welcome to join in!

As for the inside of the building, the goal is to communicate that this is a space in which holy and significant events take place, but it is a place in which you are welcome. As liturgical scholar Robert Hovda stated, "People need to be made to feel at home . . . without surrendering the worship character of the assembly. It is not merely another gathering, and the space must speak of transcendence as well as welcome."[19]

In newer church designs and in many older church rehab projects, increasing attention is being given to the foyer or narthex as a space of welcome. Larger, well-lit and comfortably decorated spaces with plenty of room for conversation communicate hospitality.

The physical space of worship is important (more will be said about this in chapter 6), but even more important is the attitude of the congregation and its leadership toward visitors and strangers. "Even when we say the right things about the Church, as the People of God," writes Hovda, "if we feel otherwise, if we feel Church is a pyramid, substantially the Pope and other bishops, or the clergy and religious, then that is the message we communicate both by the space and our manner."[20]

What Hovda is describing from his Roman Catholic perspective translates into every tradition, every congregation. If we really feel that the church is *our* church or that the church is really a clergy-dominated institution, or that this church is really only for folk like us and that other people have their own churches, then this attitude shows in the way we do or do not open up the life of the congregation to the outsider, the visitor.

A pastor of an inner-city church, one of the vital congregations studied for this book, was distressed. Called from a ministry in the suburban South to this urban congregation in the Northeast, the pastor had just led his first service of worship in his new church, and the rumors he had heard before he moved seemed to be true: this was a dying church. The congregation that Sunday was small, only a handful of folk, mostly elderly. The service plodded along with little spirit or energy. Everything seemed tired—the congregation was tired, the worship was tired; even the building, a long-neglected neo-Gothic edifice, seemed weary. There were no visitors—who would want to come?

Discouraged, the pastor walked across the street to a delicatessen and ordered a cup of coffee. Sipping his coffee, he looked over at his church, his eye wandering from the stone steps to the door to the stained-glass windows to the towers. As he surveyed the building, suddenly his imagination transformed what he was seeing. Instead of a lonely and vacant building, he began to see the church not with just one massive door but with many doors. There were large doors and small ones, doors in the front, doors along the side, and doors in the back, and people of all sorts, all ages, all conditions, and all colors were streaming through those doors into the church. He put down his coffee cup and vowed to himself, "That is what this church will become, a church with many doors wide open, welcoming all kinds of people."

The very next Sunday, the pastor told the congregation about his vision in the delicatessen and began to describe the powerful agenda for change implied in the vision. There was some inertia, some skepticism, even a little resistance, but mainly the congregation found the pastor's enthusiasm and conviction contagious, and congregants were thrilled by the infusion of energy into their moribund situation. The pastor and a few church leaders began approaching people in the neighborhood and inviting them not only to attend worship but to be an integral part of it. If the people were musicians, they were asked to play. If they were actors, they were asked to serve as lay readers. If they were dancers, they were asked to dance. The church leaders asked people not simply to come to the service, but to do something—to pray, to read, to sing, to hand out bulletins, to help prepare and serve communion. The vision, which began with the pastor alone, gradually began to be shared by the whole congregation, and a new spirit of welcome and hospitality pervaded the church. Symbolically, all the doors of the church were opened wide, and people from the neighborhood and beyond began to respond by filling up the pews on Sunday morning.

b. People want to be known by name. Not only do people want to be welcomed into the place of worship, they also want to be recognized personally. This is, first of all, a matter of being known and called by name, but it runs much deeper. To be called by one's name is a sign of being known, of coming into a community eager to discover one's story, values, and talents.

In almost all vital congregations studied, the front line of hospitality was a corps of gifted greeters. Almost every congregation has ushers, but there is a difference between an usher assigned to a duty post and someone with the holy gift of hospitality. There are people with the rare blend of memory, personality, generosity, alertness to the needs of others, and kindness who have the ability to recognize the stranger (some people shy away from greeting visitors because they are unsure who is a visitor and who is a member), to discern the proper level of greeting (some people want to be greeted with vigor while others need a quieter, unintrusive reception) and to make the stranger feel welcomed and at home. These are the people who should be given the assignment to serve as greeters; it is a ministry for which they are equipped and to which they are called. In his book *Dynamic Worship*, Kennon Callahan, an authority on church management, describes such people: "You are not looking for the backslapper or the quick-talker," he states. "You are looking for people with a quiet sense of warmth, a deep spirit of joy, and a hopeful, encouraging confidence."[21]

Callahan even recommends that, in addition to the traditional door greeters (those who stand at the entrance to the church and greet everyone), churches add an elaborate three-tier scheme of other greeters: new-person greeters (who stand back from the entrance watching for the telltale uncertainties of first-time visitors), relational ushers (ushers who personally welcome visitors and carefully seat them near regular members who have the ability to continue the welcome), and pew greeters (members seated in the congregation charged with the responsibility for welcoming visitors in a three- or four-pew section of the sanctuary.[22] "[Y]ou don't have to do all three," Callahan says. "The art is to select the one you can do best, and do that one well."[23]

In the vital churches I visited I was, in every case, warmly greeted, sometimes by an usher and sometimes by another member who happened to notice my presence. In a few instances, I was given a nametag to wear; in others I was seated and introduced by name to the others around me. The point is: I was recognized and welcomed by name.

c. People want to be joined with others in offering themselves to God in ways that truly matter. If people needed only to be warmly welcomed into church and to be recognized by name, then our goal would be simple: be a friendly church. But a key point of this chapter has been that people need more than friendliness, more than a warm welcome and a cheerful smile. People want their lives to count for something, and they come to church to make an offering. People want to join with others in giving and serving, in doing something of value for God and for the world. Symbolically, we want to place ourselves in the offering plate. The same impulse that motivates some to join the Peace Corps and others to deliver meals-on-wheels and still others to send a check for a starving child or to help build a Habitat for Humanity house or to care for a neighbor in need, is at work in every human heart. Despite the siren song of selfishness and greed that rings through the culture, people still want to give themselves away to a great and holy cause. People come to church for many reasons, but ultimately they come to offer themselves with others to God.

The vital congregations I studied all managed to communicate, as friendly and welcoming as they were, that this feeling of warmth was not an end in itself but was rather the mark of a community on the way to doing something else, something significant for God, something with weight. Many congregations are like basketball players high-fiving each other and joining hands in a show of solidarity before the game, but never moving beyond the sideline embraces to play the game. In the vital congregations, however, it was clear that we were joined in a community of hospitality but that we were also there to get on with the game.

How was this task accomplished? Partly it was a matter of the great emphasis placed on mission. All of these congregations were significantly involved in service to others, and this commitment was woven into the fabric of their worship—in announcements, prayers, sermons, and even in the hymns. One could not participate in worship in these congregations without recognizing that one was a part of a group committed to pray for and serve the world in particular ways and places. For the vital congregations, this was not a "Minute for Mission"; this was a motive for being. More will be said about the importance of mission in the vital congregations in chapter 7.

The vital congregations also invited people to offer themselves with others to God by the very structure of the worship service. As students of worship are quick to point out, a service of worship is really an event of drama, a piece of theater (we will explore the importance of this view in more detail in the next chapter). If one goes several times to a significant and complex play—say, *Hamlet* or *The Glass Menagerie*—one begins to gain a sense of what this play is *about*, what are its themes and claims upon the audience. Just so, attend a congregation's worship several times, and its core values begin to emerge. This is a subtle truth, but if worship is really only about being a warm, friendly community, then one can tell. The event turns in on itself and is never able to transcend the language of intimacy. If worship is about going to the altar and offering our lives to God, then over time one can tell that, too.

In the vital congregations, the very drama and movement of worship conveyed the idea that we were more than a collection of friends gathered for a dinner party; we were a band of pilgrims—people who knew, respected, honored, and even loved each other, but who were also on a great journey together. In one congregation, the journey led us to the pulpit, where we heard a rousing sermon summoning us to give ourselves away to God and others. In another the journey led us to the communion table of joy, where we both offered and received gifts. In still another it led us into the streets of the city, where there were places to minister and acts of kindness to perform.

Finally, the vital congregations allowed people to offer themselves in worship by recognizing and receiving the gifts that people bring. In the case of one congregation, this meant making the "tithes and offerings" element of the service itself a dramatic and powerful event. As the ushers came forward with the offering plates, the congregation followed their movements with their own bodies, turning gradually toward the altar. As the prayer of dedication was given, the plates were held high above the ushers' heads; some in the congregation raised their hands as well—a symbol of the offering of self that both included and transcended the offering of money.

However, the vital congregations did not restrict the receiving of gifts to the offering plates. In every case, the talents and abilities of the congregation were employed throughout worship. This practice included more than people singing in the choir or an occasional lay reader for the Scripture. At every point in the service the leadership of worship was shared. People in the pews sang and prayed and read and testified and blessed. The energy of worship was not concentrated in the chancel but filled the whole sanctuary. The pastor of one of these congregations said, "Things did not turn around here in worship until I learned that the most important word I could speak was yes. People would come saying, 'I have a song I would like to sing in worship' or 'I am an artist and would like to draw something for the bulletin' or 'I have done some ceramics. Is there a way they could be used in worship?' Yes, yes, yes. My job as pastor was to find a way to say the simple word yes."

Another way to think about this matter is to consider the "offering" and the "benediction" or "blessing." The offering and the benediction are elements in many services of worship, but far more than elements in the order of service, they are themes in Christian worship. People come to worship ready to make an offering, hungering to be known as persons so that they can join with others in offering themselves to God. Vital worship can happen when leaders have the wisdom to pass the plates and to receive what people have come to offer, and then to raise their hands over these offerings and to say God's word of blessing, "Yes, yes, yes."

CHAPTER 4

All the World's a Stage—
and Heaven, Too

In a memorable sermon preached by William Sloane Coffin, when he was pastor of Riverside Church in New York, he told about an annual Easter sunrise service held on the rim of the Grand Canyon. Each Easter as the first rays of the sun broke on the horizon, the words of Matthew would be read, "An angel of the Lord descended from heaven and came and rolled away the stone." Just at that moment, an enormous boulder would be pushed over the edge of the canyon, and, as the giant stone thundered down the canyon side, thousands of feet to the Colorado River below, a 2,000 voice choir would burst into Handel's "Hallelujah Chorus."

"Too dramatic?" asked Coffin. "No," he answered firmly. "[W]e live in an Easter, not a Good Friday, world."[1]

Too dramatic? To be sure, boulders are not being thrown over cliffs every Sunday, but in a time of ferment and experimentation in worship, when congregations are exploring new and sometimes daring styles and patterns of liturgy, Coffin's question is being asked with fresh urgency. Has worship in some congregations become too dramatic? Has worship become too theatrical, too performance-oriented? Theologian Marva Dawn fears so. Although she favors worship where drama and excitement grow out of a deep sense of God's presence, she is nevertheless troubled, she said, that many congregations have succumbed to a style of worship that emphasizes drama merely for the sake of drama. Such congregations produce worship that "entertains an audience instead of praising God," She warns. "Entertaining worship, she adds, is deadly to the formation of character"; she goes on to say that "we must be very careful to avoid forms of communication that dumb down or trivialize the content of our worship."[2]

The role of the dramatic in worship has always been controversial— and it should be. In a time when many church auditoriums have begun to look like television studios, when some services are constructed with the rapid episodic visual bursts of VH1, and when worship technocrats manipulate rheostats and klieg lights to manufacture liturgical "moods," it is good to warn ourselves about the dangers of making worship into a spectacle, an entertaining show for the amusement of an easily distracted crowd.

On the other hand, there is a profound sense in which authentic Christian worship is theater, and Coffin is absolutely right: the dramatic in worship grows directly out of the dramatic in the Gospel itself. In his book *Worship Is a Verb*, theological scholar Robert Webber of Wheaton College maintains that Christian worship is drama in the sense that it is both a dramatic *retelling* and a dramatic *reenactment* of the biblical story. "[W]hen I move into the sanctuary and prepare to worship," he says, "my whole body, soul, and spirit become engaged in rehearsing the work of Christ which gives shape and form to my life."[3] Effective worship involves more than plodding dutifully through of a series of prayers and hymns and recitations. Worship involves word and gesture, movement and narration, in a highly active and participatory reenactment of the Gospel story and, as such, it is inherently dramatic. As church sociologist Tex Sample has put it, "Worship is the celebration and dramatization of God's story."[4] Indeed, the third mark of the vital congregations is that they have rediscovered the authentically dramatic qualities of worship and have worked to make those qualities more evident and available to the participants:

> **CHARACTERISTIC 3.**
> VITAL AND FAITHFUL CONGREGATIONS
> HAVE RECOVERED AND MADE VISIBLE
> THE SENSE OF DRAMA
> INHERENT IN CHRISTIAN WORSHIP.

As we consider this characteristic, it is important to make a key distinction: the vital congregations did not make worship dramatic; instead they were concerned about how *to allow the drama already present* in worship to be brought to the surface and to be more deeply experienced. These congregations see worship as intrinsically dramatic, Tex Sample's "celebration and dramatization of God's story," and they seek ways to make that drama prominent and palpable. In other words, the vital congregations changed the focus of the question about the proper place of drama. Instead of asking, "Is our worship too dramatic, is it overly theatrical, or is it not dramatic enough?" they asked instead, "Does the drama in our worship genuinely spring from within the act of worship itself, that is from the Gospel being reenacted, or is it imported from the outside?" Thus, instead of worrying primarily about the intensity of the drama, they attended more to the source of the drama.

This matter of the source of drama in worship is significant. Some congregations try to jazz up worship by inserting bits of theater into the flow of worship like exclamation points—skits and film clips and helium balloons floating around the sanctuary—a sort of dramatic oregano to spice up a bland liturgical dish. But more often than not these additions are finally intrusions, interruptions, and distractions. The vital congregations, by contrast, sought to discern the dramatic qualities actually woven into the fabric of worship and to develop ways to act them out more imaginatively. As one pastor stated, "I don't have to invent my worship,"[5] because the words, the movements, the drama, the meanings are already there, present in the Gospel story.

Worship as Community Theater

Though some worshipers would be surprised to think of it this way, a service of worship is a play, a play performed in a kind of community theater. Members of a congregation are not the audience for this play (as theologian Søren Kierkegaard reminded us, *God* is the audience). The worshipers are instead the actors, and the words and actions of worship form the script for their various parts. People in a congregation come together for worship not simply to listen or to learn or to watch but to take up their roles and to act out the story of their faith. Sometimes this dramatic quality of worship is as clear as day—when, for example, a Methodist congregation acts out forgiveness and reconciliation by "passing the peace," or when in the Great Entrance in an Orthodox service the elements of the Eucharist are presented in a swirl of incense, or when a Presbyterian congregation stands up in unison to say what the church through the ages has believed by reciting the Apostles' Creed, or when a Lutheran choir, led by a crucifer holding the cross above his head, moves in procession down the center aisle singing "Lift High the Cross." At other times, the dramatic is more hidden from view, but present nonetheless. For example, when the pastor of a Nazarene church opens the Bible to read the Scripture for the day, this is not merely a matter of logistics; it is also a dramatic gesture, a part of the great play that communicates, "This is the book, this is the fountain of truth, this is the Word."

I called worship a piece of "community theater" in part because, like much community theater in other contexts, worship involves a great script being enacted by amateurs. As writer Annie Dillard delightfully describes it:

> A high school stage play is more polished than this service we have been rehearsing since the year one. In two thousand years, we have not worked out the kinks. We positively glorify them. Week after week we witness the same miracle: that God is so mighty that he can stifle his own laughter. Week after week, we witness the same miracle: that God, for reasons unfathomable, refrains from blowing our dancing bear act to smithereens. Week after week Christ washes the disciples' dirty feet, handles their very toes, and repeats, It is all right—believe it or not—to be people.[6]

As in the best community theater, the participants in worship are striving for excellence, seeking to bring their finest gifts, best skills, and most sharply honed abilities to this event. But these are not professional worshipers; they are amateurs, people who do this for love. Because this is community theater, the active involvement of every member of the community is a longed-for goal. It is more important that everybody be on the great stage speaking a part than that the parts be spoken flawlessly. It is more important that all of the singers join in the chorus than that all of the notes be true.

A friend told me about a congregation that had, as one of its ministries, a drama troupe. Several years ago, during the Christmas season, the troupe performed Dickens's *A Christmas Carol* in the fellowship hall of the church. To the delight and amusement of the congregation, one of the kindliest members of the church, an officer and respected leader, was cast in the unlikely role of the stingy curmudgeon, Ebenezer Scrooge.

In the story, you will recall, Scrooge on Christmas Eve goes through a series of terrifying and life-changing encounters with the ghosts of Christmas, experiences that cause him to repent of his cold heart and lack of generosity. As the light of Christmas Day dawns, Scrooge is a changed man.

To show this transformation, the script of the play called for the actor playing Scrooge to throw open his bedroom window, to stick his head out into
the light, to act as though he saw a lad walking along the street, and to
beckon with joy and excitement to the imaginary boy, "Hey boy, boy, you
there. Come up here. I have something for you to do." Then Scrooge was
to distribute gifts for the poor of London.

In the actual performance, though, when the actor thrust his head through
the window of the set and said, "Hey boy, boy, you there," a young boy in
the fellowship hall, sitting with his parents and watching the play, thought
that Scrooge was speaking personally to him. So, when the actor said, "Come
up here. I have something for you to do," the boy obediently got out of his
seat and walked onto the stage. Suddenly and unexpectedly, there in the
middle of the play was a child from the audience. At that point, the roles of
Christian and church officer overcame the role of "Scrooge," and the actor
spontaneously went over to the boy and hugged him, saying, "Yes, indeed,
you are the one I need, the very one." When the play was over, the cast
was applauded enthusiastically, but none more warmly than Scrooge and
the little boy.

This is a parable of Christian worship. We are all actors in a great play,
and the script of the Gospel drama repeatedly beckons to those sitting in the
bleachers, standing on the periphery, existing on the margins: "Come up
here. I have something for you to do." And so it happens that there on
stage, week after week, are those who have not yet mastered their lines,
who have not yet fully learned the lyrics, but who have found themselves
beckoned by the very drama of worship itself into the middle of the action.

This dramatic, involving, beckoning dimension of worship is so woven
into the fabric of a service that it can be obscured, even lost altogether. If
we do not attend to it and highlight it, it can recede into the background and
be hidden from view. When this happens, worship loses some of its capacity to generate wonder and its power to involve the participants in its action.
How then can this sense of drama be restored?

DRAMATIC STRUCTURE

The first step in recovering the dramatic sense of Christian worship is to
make sure that the service of worship flows well, which requires that the
order of worship be strong and logically constructed. A service of worship

consists of a variety of elements—such as prayers, Scripture readings, a sermon, and hymns—placed in some kind of sequence, an *order* of worship. Even congregations in the free-church traditions, congregations that prize spontaneity, avoid prayer books, print no bulletins, and resist being constrained by fixed liturgies—even such congregations nevertheless have an ordered worship. Attend such a church once and the service seems to flow unpredictably, the wind of the Spirit blowing where it will, but go back a dozen times and the repeated patterns and structural constants begin to emerge.

These patterns and sequences — whether they be the rhythms of *The Book of Common Prayer* or the "sing, pray, preach, have-an-altar-call" blueprint of the independent evangelical church—are not ruts; they are embodied convictions. The shape of worship conveys meaning. The order of worship is an implicit narrative, although its narrative shape may be partially hidden from view. Underlying every coherent act of worship is a sacred story, and the sequence of elements in worship is, in effect, a retelling of that story.

Consider, for example, the typical fourfold pattern of worship employed by many traditions: Gathering, Word, Eucharist, Sending. This structure is not just an orderly way to organize the service; it actually tells a story that goes something like this: In the midst of our life in the world, we are called into God's presence. There in awe and wonder, praise and confession, we are spoken to by God; called afresh to be God's people; given encouragement, wisdom, forgiveness, and healing; and invited to come to the heavenly banquet where, in the spirit of thanksgiving, we join the saints of all times and places in a great feast of joy. Then, having been fed by God, we are sent back into the world as people renewed, to love and serve in God's name.

That is one version of the sacred Christian story, but not the only one that can be told. Other services move not to the table but to an "invitation" to believe, a call to those who are not part of the Christian faith to repent and confess the Gospel and to come forward to show their new faith. These services retell the sacred story of a God who seeks and saves the lost. Still other services follow the sermon with a time of discussion, meditation, even debate. These services tell the sacred story of a God whose truth takes root in our hearts and minds.

The point is that many different orders of worship are used in Christian churches, but in all of them good worship is an acted-out story, a piece of community theater. Indeed, one of the tests of worship is whether the order of worship can be narrated. If we cannot take the elements of the order of worship—hymn of praise, prayer of confession, Scripture, and so on—and recount the story implied in their ordering, then there are missing elements or the elements are out of proper sequence.

Having a good narrative order is not enough, though. Congregations often experience worship as a series of disconnected elements—hymn, prayer, announcements, reading, sermon, hymn—next, next, next. The responsibility falls on the leaders of worship to conduct the service in such a way that the connections among the elements are clear, that the narrative flow of the service is evident. In the vital churches I observed, the leaders of worship (clergy, lay leaders, musicians) seemed keenly aware of the flow of the service and allowed their leadership to be governed by it. Mostly this was a matter of pacing. When something happened in worship that had dramatic impact—whether an anthem, a sermon, a declaration, or a dance—often the pace of the service would slow, giving time for this element to be absorbed and reflected upon. At other times, though, the pace would quicken when an element of worship was a direct and immediate response to the previous one (such as a musical element of praise and thanksgiving after the words of pardon or a hymn of dedication after a sermon calling for commitment). Like all good narratives, services of worship contain various internal pacings and matters of timing, and effective worship leaders can convey the fact that the contours of the service move up and down and that this element grows out of the one before and leads logically to the next one.

Enlivening the Scenes

As a whole, a worship service reenacts the story of the Gospel, and, as we have already described, this dramatic whole is divided into several discrete scenes, such as the gathering scene, the proclamation of the Word scene, the Lord's Supper scene, and the sending forth into the world scene. The vital congregations not only emphasized the overall flow and dramatic structure of the service; they also paid attention to the dramatic potential of the individual scenes.

For example, one of the vital congregations gave particular dramatic intensity to the gathering scene. This is an Episcopal congregation, and its service begins every week with a processional of choir and clergy, moving from the narthex into the nave of the church, down the aisle to the chancel, singing the opening hymn accompanied by the organ. Nothing unusual about that; the same is done in many other churches. This congregation, however, has a large number of West Indians among the membership, Anglican in tradition but Caribbean in culture. So some choir singers carry not only hymnals but also tambourines and maracas. The procession does not make a beeline right down the center aisle, it wanders in serpentine fashion, moving joyfully and on a somewhat unpredictable path through the nave, pausing occasionally among the congregants to sway to the opening hymn as the choir and clergy wind their way gradually toward the chancel. The experience for this congregation is obviously quite different than it would be if the choir did the traditional straight-line procession. One does not have the sense, "Well, here come the choir and clergy." One rather has the sense of an event about to happen, of being gathered up in a joyful throng heading toward the temple for worship, spirits rising as we go.

Another of the vital congregations, a Lutheran church, was effective in allowing the intrinsic drama of baptism to shine through. The traditional service from the *Lutheran Book of Worship* was used, but much thought was taken to allow the actions and signs of this service to be visible and meaningful. The whole event was carefully choreographed—so carefully, in fact, that it did not seem "staged"; it moved with apparent naturalness and ease. The parents of the child to be baptized gathered in the front with the clergy and lay leaders. The words of the service were spoken with conviction. Though these words were read from the service book, the effect of this reading was to say, "We are being obedient to a tradition with which we are deeply familiar," rather than, "We are reading some difficult material from a book." The baptism itself was accomplished with a highly visible and audible display—the sight of water being poured and the sound of water splashing in the font. A small baptismal garment, a white stole, was lovingly placed on the child, the new garment of salvation. Hands were laid upon the child, as a sign of her becoming one of God's holy people, the sign of the cross was made with joy, and a Christ candle was placed in the hands of the parents.

Then something quite remarkable happened. Sometimes at this point in a baptismal service, well-meaning ministers will pick up the newly baptized infant and walk around the sanctuary, smiling, saying warm things, and showing the child to members of the congregation. The intention is noble, but it rarely comes off well. Most of the time it serves to communicate mainly that the baby is cute and that the pastor is a fine and tender person—good thoughts, to be sure, but a narrative about Gerber babies and nice pastors is not the story being told in baptism. This action is a perfect example of a finally distracting drama imported from outside the Gospel and imposed upon worship.

This Lutheran congregation did something markedly different, a dramatic enactment that was not a piece of theater imposed on the event but a true expression of the story being told in baptism. When the baptism was complete, the baptismal party moved together down the center aisle of the church. The clergy and lay leaders carried the Bible and the prayer book. The newly baptized child was wearing the baptismal stole, and the group was led by the parents, one carrying the baby and the other carrying the lighted Christ candle. As they moved up the aisle from the front, another group came down the aisle toward them from the rear—the children of the congregation together with some members of a sister congregation in Guatemala who happened to be visiting that day. As the two groups met in mid-aisle, literally in the midst of the congregation, the children and the Christians from Guatemala led the congregation in a greeting for the baptized child: "We welcome you into the Lord's family. We receive you as a fellow member of the body of Christ, a child of the same heavenly Father, and a worker with us in the kingdom of God." The congregation broke into spontaneous applause as gifts, including a Bible and a baptismal certificate, were presented to the child as a sign that the whole church, both in this place and throughout the world, was welcoming this new member into participation in the body of Christ.

Another of the vital congregations, an African-American church in Chicago, also underscored the dramatic power of worship in a "baby dedication." At the appropriate point in the service, the pastor called the families of the babies to be dedicated to the front of the church. The sanctuary was designed as a semicircle, and there was a large open space in front of the chancel steps, which quickly filled with people. About 20 babies were being dedicated, and coming forward with them were not only their parents but also grandparents, aunts and uncles, cousins, neighbors, and friends. Suddenly there were a couple of hundred people at the front of the church, surrounding the babies and their parents.

The pastor moved calmly and deliberately from baby to baby, taking his time, ensuring that every child was treated with great importance. "What is the name of this child?" the pastor would ask, and the mother would say the child's first name, the father would announce the child's middle name, and the whole cluster of family and friends would shout out the child's last name—an audible sign that this child was the coming together of several streams of heritage and identity. The pastor would then bless each child by name.

When the pastor had blessed the last child, African drums began to beat rhythmically. The parents and their babies marched to the beat across the front of the sanctuary and up the steps into the broad chancel area, as the drums grew more insistent and the congregation joined in with cries of praise and thanksgiving. When the parents and their children were arrayed across the chancel and as the drums continued to strike the rhythm, a team of women, lay worship leaders, began to move from child to child, each woman carrying something to place in the mouths of the babies. The first woman placed a bit of pepper in each baby's mouth, and as she did a woman at the lectern said, "This pepper is a sign of the power of the cross." The next woman put a drop of water in each mouth. "This water is a sign of the purity of Christ, to whom this child belongs." The next woman placed a pinch of salt on the tongues of the children. "This salt is a sign that these children are called to be wise and faithful, the salt of the earth." The next woman carried drops of vinegar, and the babies winced. "This vinegar is a sign that the Christian life will not always be easy and that these children must be prepared to face difficulties and suffering." The next a bit of honey. "A sign of the sweetness of the Gospel." The last woman carried oil. "A sign of joy."

When the women had finished, the drums grew very loud, the congregation rose with acclamations to its feet, and the parents lifted up each child as high as they could over their heads as the woman at the lectern announced with joyful triumph, "These children were not born into slavery. They are the free children of the heavenly King, those loved and chosen by God most High!" It was a moment of great power and drama, a moment of witness to the Gospel.

The authentic and faithful dramatic possibilities in Christian worship are almost infinite. A Catholic parish with a mass in both Spanish and English uses simple pictures, hand-drawn done on poster board, to accompany the sermon and to make its meaning visible regardless of language. A Methodist congregation joins hands in a large circle around the communion table as worshipers observe Holy Communion. A Baptist congregation, at the time of the "pastoral prayer," invites those in special need of prayer to come and stand with the minister at the front of the church as the rest of congregation stands and surrounds them with prayer and loving support. A Presbyterian congregation occasionally invites every member who plays a musical instrument to bring it to worship and to join in the accompaniment of the hymns, a symbol of the gifts of God's people being gathered, celebrated, and employed.

Every congregation has the opportunity to think through the dramatic narrative of its service of worship and to ask at each point along the way, "Is there a way to allow the inherent drama in this scene to be more fully visible, to be more completely clear in its meaning, and to be more inviting to participation?" The result will be worship full of action, an event of Gospel community theater generating excitement and summoning people out of their seats and onto center stage.

Too dramatic? No. After all, we live in an Easter world!

CHAPTER 5

O for a Thousand Tongues: The Challenge of Music

Music is the nuclear reactor of congregational worship. It is where much of the radioactive material is stored, where a good bit of the energy is generated, and, alas, where congregational meltdown is most likely to occur. Change the order of worship, and you may set off a debate. Change the style of music, and you may split the congregation. "Our new sectarianism is a sectarianism of worship style," writes Notre Dame history professor Michael S. Hamilton. "The new sectarian creeds are dogmas of music."[1]

Why is it that music, gentle music, is one of the most volatile and controversial issues in worship? Some argue that our tensions over music are just one more manifestation of the broader culture wars, especially those fought along generational battle lines. Each generation, it is said, has its own musical preferences and that trying to get a 16-year-old to enjoy singing "The Church's One Foundation" is like trying to get rockers and rappers like Metallica or Eminem to croon "I believe for every drop of rain that falls, a flower grows."

Sociologist of religion Tex Sample tells a story about music and the generations that he sees as a parable of the church.[2] The story concerns a midwestern shopping mall designed to have a nostalgic appeal to older, more affluent shoppers—quaint gaslights, gourmet restaurants, boutiques with cute awnings and expensive goods. But the winds of culture blow where they will, and for some mysterious reason this mall is discovered by the city's teenagers and becomes the cool place to hang out. Every night young people crowd the walkways and the stores, and the constant circling of their cars makes the parking lot almost impossible to navigate. They come, but they don't buy. The teenagers jam the mall for the event of being where the action is, not for the merchandise, and the mall's business falls off precipitously. The merchants, faced with a perilous dilemma, come up with a brilliant idea: play "easy listening" music over the mall's sound system. When they do, the young people swiftly flee, never to return.

This story, Sample declares, is a warning sign for "churches that will not bother to learn and practice the soul musics of the great majority of people in this culture."[3] By holding firm to Bach-bred anthems and "easy listening" traditional hymns, the church repels young people and risks permanently alienating a whole generation.

Others disagree that music is so generationally linked, pointing out that musical preferences are more a matter of exposure, training, and personal taste than they are a product of mere chronological age. As one church member put it, "They say baby boomers don't like traditional hymns. Well, I'm a boomer, and I love the old hymns." It also seems true that teenagers who sing in highly disciplined choirs at school or church are often far more likely to appreciate Bach and Haydn than are their peers. On the other side of the generational ledger, at a church conference recently I met a man in his 70s who handed me a brochure for an upcoming concert of praise music. It turns out that this fellow, bored in worship all his life, had finally, to his liberation and delight, stumbled across a church whose worship featured praise choruses sung by the worshipers, hands waving over their heads, to the driving beat of a electric-guitar-fueled rock band and to lyrics flashed on an overhead screen. This septuagenarian had never worshiped so passionately in all his life. As pioneer rock 'n' roll artist Chuck Berry once sang, "'C'est la vie,' say the old folks, it goes to show you never can tell."

Underneath all of the questions and debates about music, generations, and taste lies the more basic truth that we tend to find ourselves so often in conflict over music in worship because, regardless of our age or situation, music is so very powerful and formative in religious experience. It was probably only a slight exaggeration when one church musician suggested that we get our theology far more often from the hymns we sing than from the sermons we hear. We would not fight so vigorously over music if it did not mean so much to us, and this meaning resides at levels often difficult to articulate.

Take, for example, the experience of a committee putting together a new, revised hymnal for a large denomination. When the group announced that it was considering dropping the hymn "Onward, Christian Soldiers" because of its militaristic imagery, the negative reaction was quick and vigorous. I daresay, if the committee had announced that it was thinking of removing a clause from the Nicene Creed, hardly a ripple would have stirred the waters, but when it proposed taking away a beloved hymn, a tsunami of protest arose.

Now, if the defenders of "Onward, Christian Soldiers" had been asked, "Do you really think we ought to be singing about warfare in church? Is that what Jesus desires?" probably a good measure of them would have said "No, but that doesn't make any difference because that's not what 'Onward, Christian Soldiers' is about." To be sure, arguing that a hymn that begins "Onward, Christian soldiers, marching as to war" is not about warfare is something of a tough putt, but there is at least a partial sense in which these defenders would be correct. An old hymn that folk have been singing in church and camp and Bible school and maybe even while they weed the garden is now so full of emotional associations, memories, and intertextual linkages that a supercomputer could not crunch all the meanings. Singing a well-known and well-loved hymn means a thousand things, at every level possible, and all at once. Taking away a hymn like that is an editorial and theological issue for some; for others it is a heart transplant.

Tex Sample again has a fitting story, this time showing how hymns work at multiple levels of human experience. It seems that Sample, in one of his classes, had been lampooning the old hymn "In the Garden." Musically, this hymn does invite ridicule. It is syrupy sweet, escapist, and irredeemably individualistic ("I come to the garden alone, while the dew is still on the roses"), and what is more, it is set to an insipid, sentimental, and cliché-ridden tune. Sample was having fun with all this, sending up the hymn by singing a parody of it for his class, using his most whiny, nasal voice. However, when the class ended, a 35-year-old woman in the class approached Sample privately and told him that her father had sexually abused her from the time she was 11 until she was 16, at which point she had found the strength to put a stop to it. After every terrible incident, she had gone outside the house and sung, "I come to the garden alone, while the dew is still on the roses. . . . And he walks with me and he talks with me, and he tells me I am his own." She told Sample, "Without that song, I don't know how I could have survived. Tex, don't . . . you . . . ever . . . ever . . . make fun of that song in my presence again."[4]

A person's music is a powerful alloy of memory and emotion, experience and conviction, expression and aspiration. No wonder feelings are aroused, defenses mounted, and passionate arguments ignited whenever the topic of music and worship is raised.

A Tale of Two Services

To get a sense of the troop movements in the battle over music in worship, consider the case of Middletown Church, whose experience is increasingly typical. Five years ago, Middletown Church was a struggling Protestant congregation with a traditional 11 A.M. Sunday service and gradually decaying attendance patterns. A group of younger adults in the congregation, many of whom had experienced new styles of worship at a conferences and in other churches, reported to the pastor and officers that they were bored with Middletown's worship and asked for permission to start a "contemporary" alternative service.

After some hesitation, the officers agreed to allow an experiment: for six months the church would have two Sunday services, a "contemporary" service at 9:30 A.M. and a "traditional" service at 11 A.M. After six months, a judgment would be made as to whether the two services would continue. Now, five years later, the early service is still going strong, and as a result, two very distinct worship constituencies with different values and tastes in worship have been formed in the Middletown congregation.

Sunday morning at Middletown goes like this: Before 8 A.M. a small volunteer work crew begins to set up the sanctuary for the 9:30 service. The pulpit, communion table, and baptismal font are moved to a storeroom, and in their place go a giant screen, an overhead projector, two drum sets, a bevy of guitars, and a control board connected to an elaborate network of stage lights and a concert-sized sound system. By 9:15, the sanctuary is nearly filled, mainly (but not exclusively) with casually dressed people in their teens, 20s, and 30s, and the musicians, some of them wearing Garth Brooks–style headset microphones, have begun to warm up the gathering with a few impromptu praise choruses.

The first service lasts until 10:30 or so, at which point the members of the work crew urgently and somewhat noisily take down the screen, drums, lights, and speakers and quickly replace the regular sanctuary furniture. Some of the 11:00 A.M. worshipers, who are on the whole grayer than the early crowd and clothed mostly in business suits and smart dresses, have been huddled in the narthex, waiting their chance to enter the sanctuary. As the two congregations pass each other like high-schoolers in the hallway between classes, there are a few disapproving glances, a scattering of greetings, and a whole lot of silence.

There are similarities between the two services. Both have prayers, singing, Scripture readings, an offering, and a benediction. The minister preaches basically the same sermon at both services. Both include baptisms on occasion, and both incorporate the Lord's Supper about a dozen times a year. But there are big differences, too. The early service is much more informal, much more energetic, and much better attended. Because there is no pulpit, the minister preaches from the floor level wearing a lapel microphone and sometimes moving around among the congregation. Applause and laughter are heard far more frequently at the early service, and the prayers are spoken extemporaneously, sometimes with a clumsiness of language and a meandering style, but always with earnestness and heartfelt conviction.

The main difference, however, between the two services—the difference that finally forces people to choose one service over the other—is the music. At the early service, there are guitars, drums, and tambourines. At the later service there is the pipe organ, supplemented on festival occasions by brass. At the later service a professional musician serves as organist and choirmaster, and a choir with trained soloists sings at least one anthem every Sunday, drawn from a repertoire of pieces chosen by the choirmaster for their musical and theological merit.

At the early service, there is a band, musically talented but not trained. Most of the time, the band leads congregational singing, but occasionally the players perform a song on their own. At the later service there are always three hymns: an opening hymn of praise, a middle hymn often on the theme of the sermon, and a closing, going-out-into-the-world hymn. At the early service, there is a great deal more music—at least half of the worship time is spent singing—but only rarely is there a recognizable "hymn"; most of the time the music consists of praise songs and choruses.

The fact is, if the music were removed, there would be hardly a dime's worth of difference between the two services. Boiled down to essentials, then, the choice is between traditional church music—hymns in the hymnbook augmented by anthems sung by the choir—and what has come to be known as "praise music." Praise music forms a notoriously difficult genre to define, but some of hymn writer Brian Wren's descriptive phrases are helpful. Much of praise music, he states, consists of what he calls "evangelical choruses." An evangelical chorus is "a short congregational song that states its theme without developing it, in words and music designed for easy singing, repetition, and 'uplift'";[5] such choruses are usually based on biblical quotes or allusions and often place "the singer in direct, personal, loving relationship with God, or Jesus";[6] the driving beat of these choruses is an essential feature, creating a palpable effect on the worshipers and "inviting congregational hand-clapping and body movement."[7]

An outsider looking at Middletown Church would have to conclude that the future belongs to the early service. Not only is that service filled with worshipers and charged with energy; it shows bursts of imagination and creativity, manages to develop real congregational participation, and has been instrumental in drawing many people from outside the Christian faith into the Christian fold. In comparison, the later service seems tired, in-grown, and somewhat dispirited. Not unexpectedly, many of the 11 A.M. crowd grumble about the early service. It is, they complain, noisy, irrever-ent, and mostly show, and the setting up and tearing down of the equipment is disrespectful to the sanctuary and disruptive to worshipers who attend the later service. "It's a fad," one long-time Middletown member says of the early service. "Give it a few more years, and it will have blown over. They'll be back with us at 11."

Much of this grumbling sounds like the normal crankiness of human beings trying to live together in close space and with competing needs and desires. However, the early service, for all of its seeming virtues, has its sharper critics as well.

IT'S ONLY ROCK 'N' ROLL, BUT I HATE IT

It is fairly easy to see what is wrong with the 11 A.M. service. It is stale, remote, inhospitable, and boring. It is clearly on a respirator and, unless something drastic happens, a funeral for it can be planned. But many expe-rienced church musicians would cast a wary eye toward Middletown's early service as well. While acknowledging, even admiring, its energy, imagina-tion, and magnetic appeal, they would argue that, in the long run, such a service could well turn out to be not a service at all, but, ironically, a disser-vice. The problem, as they would see it, is almost entirely in the music. Middletown's early service is built around bad church music, they would argue, and consistently bad music in worship leads to stunted development in faith.

What is wrong with the music at Middletown's early service? After all, it's joyful and easy to sing, and its driving beat almost compels congrega-tional participation and whole-body involvement. Aren't those desirable qualities? Yes, say the critics, but typical praise music is also simplistic, repetitive, and, finally, boring (one observer of church life, no fan of praise music, quipped, "A praise song—four words, three chords, two hours"). In the short run, it gets you on your feet clapping your hands, but in the long run it cultivates a monotonic, downsized faith, a faith too naïve and simple to handle complexity, too repetitive to deal with real change.

A London music critic commented a few years back about the strange and telling experience he had the day of Princess Diana's funeral. He was present for the funeral at Westminster Abbey but left soon after the service to travel across town for a performance that evening of Verdi's *Requiem*. In a few hours, then, he moved from the emotional throb of the huge crowd at the funeral, sobbing as Elton John sang the pop lament "Goodbye, England's Rose," to the rich, majestic, and intricate funeral mass of Verdi. As he drove home from the concert, he mused about the differences in the two events. Both were powerful emotional, social, and religious experiences, he realized, and in both cases the meaning and emotions rode largely on the carrier wave of the music. But he finally decided that what the music of Verdi possessed that Elton John's tribute lacked was *awe*, the sense that one was being taken into the presence of great and holy mystery. Indeed, it is this lack of awe, this tendency, however emotionally rousing, to remain earthbound, that critics find most telling in contemporary praise music. Music professor Thomas Day goes after contemporary pop church music with a blunt object: "[T]hose casual, la-dee-da melodies, the easy familiarity of the music, and the let-me-show-you-how-sincere-I-am expressiveness all indicate that God is our *little* friend. . . . As one music critic has put it, the music seems to say, . . . 'Have a nice day, God.'"[8]

Moreover, say the critics, much of what passes for contemporary worship music is almost exclusively self-centered, or worse. Again, Thomas Day has little use for it: "[T]he problem with this music: simply put, nearly all of it—no matter how sincere, no matter how many scriptural texts it contains—oozes with an indecent narcissism."[9]

Is this fair? To be sure, there is plenty of "I" and "me" language in praise music, but is not this about the "I" who praises God? And isn't there plenty of "I" and "me" language in traditional hymnody? These are complicated questions, say the critics. Yes, the "I" and "me" in praise music is mostly about praising God, but the real energy is falls upon the "me," the one doing the praising and the feeling. Hymn writer Brian Wren has attempted to capture the inherent solipsism of praise music in a whimsical parody of a praise chorus:

Oh, I'm thinking of me praising Jesus,
and loving the feeling I feel.
    When I think of his touch
    I am feeling so much
that tomorrow I'll praise him for real.[10]

As for the "I" and "me" references in traditional hymnody, there is, one must admit, excessive individualism in the texts of some hymns, especially those coming from the piety of the 19th century, but even these hymns, say the defenders of traditional church music, are often set to tunes that make it clear musically that this song is being sung in public worship. The focus on the personal in the lyrics is mediated by a tune that supports communal singing. In other words, the lyrics say "I," but the music says "we."[11]

So the battle continues. On the one side, many trained church musicians are aware of the great theological depth and musical treasures in the church's wide repertoire and are as heartsick about the trivialities of contemporary worship music as many preachers are about the low-calorie, self-help bromides that pass for sermons in many churches these days. On the other hand, the praise and contemporary music advocates can point to the rousing success and overwhelming popularity of services with high-energy music. Times are changing, they say, and musical styles change with them. Attempts to build a high wall of protection around the old churchly repertoire are shortsighted, elitist, and destined to further empty the pews of already failing congregations. Where should we turn for help?

WHEN IN OUR MUSIC GOD IS GLORIFIED

Amazingly, the vital congregations observed for this book have managed to find a way through, a "third way," on the difficult issue of music as well.

CHARACTERISTIC 4.

VITAL AND FAITHFUL CONGREGATIONS
EMPHASIZE CONGREGATIONAL MUSIC
THAT IS BOTH EXCELLENT AND ECLECTIC
IN STYLE AND GENRE.

It is important to recognize that all three components of this characteristic—congregational, excellent, and eclectic—are crucial to understanding how these congregations approach music.

Congregational

As is the case with many congregations today, the vital congregations include large servings of congregational music in their worship. This may seem obvious and natural, but it is actually a quite remarkable trend. Music in worship rises and falls in importance in Christian history. For example, in the medieval period, singing in worship slipped away from congregations in many places and into the mouths of the clergy only. The Reformation generally burst forth with congregational song. However, Ulrich Zwingli of Zurich, who was by most accounts the most gifted musician among the Reformers, was suspicious of music's power to seduce and, therefore, eliminated all musical instruments from Lord's Day worship. In my own Presbyterian tradition, we speak proudly of how the congregational singing of the Psalms is a treasured part of our heritage. Even so, history discloses many small congregations of Scottish Presbyterians where actual singing in worship was so undervalued that they knew only three or four bland tunes, to which they sang all of the metrical psalms. Music comes and goes in importance.

On the surface, then, the vital congregations represent a trend toward the increased use of music in worship. But the shift is more than quantity. While some churches may see worship as a series of words punctuated occasionally by pieces of music—a hymn, a response, an interlude—in the vital congregations one has the sense of being carried along in the service by music, of music as the thread that ties the flow of the service together. There is simply a lot of music in the worship of these congregations, and it is used in a variety of ways. Full-length hymns and shorter choruses are employed to gather the people, to reinforce the reading of Scripture and the preaching, to generate a sense of mystery throughout, to cultivate congregational participation, to express thanksgiving and joy, to surround the offerings of the people, and to send the congregation into the world to service.

Most of the vital congregations have choirs and professional musicians on staff, but the emphasis definitely falls upon congregational music rather than the offerings of highly skilled musicians. There was no sense at any point in the worship that the congregation was an audience listening to a performance by the choir, or sitting quietly in the sanctuary to hear and applaud an organ postlude. Indeed, some of these congregations strongly place the emphasis not upon the trained musicians but upon the rich variety of musical gifts distributed throughout the whole church. During the offering, members of some of these congregations sing and play brass, strings, guitars, dulcimers, woodwinds, or whatever else they have the gift to play. Even when choirs are involved, there is no feeling that the service has come to a halt while the choir "does" an anthem. Rather, the choral music falls naturally into the flow of worship. The choirs advance the movement of the service and give voice to thoughts and emotions shared by the whole congregation. Thus, the congregations do not listen to the music; they listen and worship *with* it.

Excellent

Standards of musical excellence are hard to define, but not impossible, Just as there is good and bad writing, there is good and bad music. Most musicians would agree, for example, that the hymn "For All the Saints," set to the Vaughan Williams tune *Sine Nomine*, is musically and poetically superior to "Blessed Assurance, Jesus is Mine!" set to Phoebe Palmer Knapp's tune *Assurance*. The former hymn has a more complex and interesting melody and richer harmony, and the lyrics are more profound theologically (the Methodist theologian H. E. Luccock once quipped that, instead of "Blessed assurance, Jesus is mine!" the hymn would be more apt theologically if it were "Blessed disturbance, we are his!"). But even if we could agree that "For All the Saints" is inherently a more excellent hymn than "Blessed Assurance," does that make "For All the Saints" a better hymn for worship? If a congregation can and will sing "Blessed Assurance" with passion, but sits glumly and silently through "For All the Saints," then doesn't the sheer fact that one hymn works and the other does not reshuffle the deck on musical excellence?

Yes and no. The first mark of musical excellence in worship is a functional one. Good music is that which empowers the congregation and gives the congregation a means to express the thoughts and feelings of their worship. If a hymn or other musical piece is beyond a congregation's range or reach, then it cannot be called excellent, no matter how superb it may be on internal and technical grounds. On the other hand, this does not mean that every hymn a congregation enjoys singing is excellent. Some music sung or played with exuberance is sentimental, trivial, and unworthy of worship. To be truly excellent, music in worship must pass two tests: functional and internal. The music of worship should be good music as measured by inherent musical standards, and it should be effective music as measured by how well it actually works in a given congregation to give voice and expression to praise.

This balance between use and intrinsic merit is not easy to strike, of course. One of the wisest descriptions I have heard of how to achieve the balance came from the hymnologist Eric Routley. At a conference, he was asked the perennial question about popular taste versus musical excellence. "Should the church musician allow the congregation to sing the hymns they know and love or should the musician demand that they sing better music?" In other words, should congregations be permitted to sing what they like or should they be required to sing what's good for them? Routley, a superb church musician, surprised the group by responding, "You have to begin with what a congregation knows and likes, with what they will sing. But the church musician must always put a little musical pressure on the congregation to move them along into more mature musical expression. You begin where they are, but you don't leave them there." Routley's view is quite helpful; what counts for musical excellence in worship is music in which we can genuinely participate but which also encourages us to grow into more mature and complex understandings of faith. The best hymn is one the congregation can sing with passion but which also leaves the worshipers changed at the end.[12]

This dual concern for function and quality was present in the vital congregations. The music of hymns and responses was almost uniformly excellent. There were no repetitive praise choruses, no cliché-ridden hymns. On the other hand, none of the music was so complex that it silenced all but the musical experts in the congregation. Every musical piece was "singer-friendly."

Eclectic

One of the most remarkable features of the music in the vital congregation is how varied it is in style and genre. Often this variety can be experienced in a single service—a Taizé chorus followed by an early American hymn; "Lift High the Cross" in the same service as "Shalom, My Friend"; a Reformation baptism hymn nestled together with a spiritual and "Shall We Gather at the River"—but mainly the eclectic range occurs over time, through the week-in, week-out worship life of the congregation. If one attends one of these vital congregations over many weeks, one experiences an amazing diversity of music—from classical to folk, from Bach to rock.

If we think of the repertoire of church music as a spectrum, from traditional at one end of the scale to contemporary and *avant-garde* at the other, most congregations draw vertical lines defining their desired bandwidth. "We do this kind of music, but not those kinds," they say. The vital congregations, however, did not draw vertical lines, but a horizontal one. Above the line is excellence, below the line is inferior music, and the vital congregations sought musical excellence across a broad range of musical idioms.

A Gift of Song

Putting this all together, then, when one enters the sanctuary of a vital congregation, one encounters music, and plenty of it. The congregation sings and plays musical instruments, and music holds the service together from beginning to end. The music is selected out of alertness to the moment in worship—a vigorous hymn of praise here, a reflective lament or a hopeful chorus there. The styles vary, and music from all eras of the church's history—from ancient Jewish chants to Latin American rhythms—is employed.

This is not to say that there are no rough edges. Not everyone likes every form of music, and an ethic of tolerance and mutual participation is required. People need to be willing to sing music they do not necessarily like for the sake of the unity of the body. Or again, in one of the vital churches, a member of the congregation announced that he had a musical offering he would like to share. What followed was a sentimental, overdramatic presentation of an old favorite hymn from the man's childhood. It was a bad piece of music, but the congregation listened with love and genuine appreciation as he sang. The music was hardly worth a dime, but the offering was the "widow's mite," thankfully given and joyfully received.

CHAPTER 6

Tents, Temples, and Tables:
The Space of Worship

The good news about church architecture is that a congregation's vision and conviction about worship are embodied in its buildings. Unfortunately, this is often the bad news about church architecture, too, since subsequent generations must live in these buildings and participate in these visions, even when understandings of how we worship change. A church's worship space—whether it be a storefront room with folding chairs on a busy city street, a Romanesque building dominating the countryside, or a cozy meeting house of warm wood and glass nestled into a natural setting—bears silent and reliable witness to how that church contemplates the encounter between God and humanity in worship. But when attitudes toward worship modify and reform, buildings do not easily reform with them. In fact, so many substantial changes in worship have occurred in the last generation in preaching, music, congregational involvement, the role of clergy, and other areas—that one major book on church architecture maintains that these shifts "have made partially obsolete all churches built before 1970, and quite a number since."[1]

I once worshiped in an otherwise lovely college chapel built in the late 1950s that had, to put it mildly, a weird pulpit. The pulpit was not at the front in the chancel area but was located in a balcony attached to a side wall. It was some 30 feet above floor level. At sermon time, the preacher would open a door leading to this balcony and suddenly appear on this minaret-like perch, three stories above contradiction, as the congregation craned its necks upward to see and hear.

There is an explanation. The college is related to a Protestant denomination with an extraordinarily high theology of preaching, and the idea behind this vaulted pulpit was, of course, to symbolize the Word that comes to earth from on high. Unfortunately, by the time the 1960s rolled around, attitudes about worship and authority had shifted, and the pulpit signified to most students who came to chapel not the Word coming from on high but the clergy coming from outer space, hopelessly hierarchical, remote, and out of touch. Any preacher foolish enough to pop out onto that balcony, like a cuckoo in a tower clock, would have been subject to ridicule. So a portable lectern was placed on the floor level for speaking and preaching, and the balcony pulpit gathers cobwebs to this day. (However, views about worship are sure to keep changing, and there may come a day in a future we cannot yet imagine when the cobwebs will be swept away and that lofty pulpit reclaimed with a triumphant shout and head-shaking wonder that people ever could have so unspiritual to have abandoned it.)

When attitudes toward worship change, some congregations have the luxury of building new worship spaces for new times, but given the price of construction, most churches will have to make do with their present "obsolete" buildings. This necessity can be a real deterrent to worship reform, since buildings can make us feel trapped in the patterns of worship for which they were designed. When, for example, the sanctuary is built like a railroad car, with rows of fastened-down pews all facing forward, how can a congregation do anything other than the clergy-centered, chancel-focused, listen-to-the-preacher-talk style of worship captured in that floor plan?[2]

In this regard, it is significant that all of the vital congregations observed for this book made creative use of their worship space, but only one of these congregations worships in a sanctuary built after 1970. The rest of them have had to struggle with all of the usual constraints of older buildings—indeed, in one case, a sanctuary that has sections nearly 250 years old. For the most part, they have not knocked down walls or built new wings. They have instead worked with light and color; they have cleared out clutter and placed a piece of furniture here rather than there; they have taken the structures they inherited and, through a hundred little modifications, allowed those buildings to support the dynamics of worship. Their buildings do not give them complete freedom, but these congregations have nevertheless found ways to bend what they cannot break, leading to this mark of vital and faithful worship:

> ### CHARACTERISTIC 5.
> VITAL AND FAITHFUL CONGREGATIONS
> CREATIVELY ADAPT
> THE SPACE AND ENVIRONMENT OF WORSHIP.

To say that the vital congregations creatively adapt their worship spaces does not mean that they give unfettered reign to their interior-decorator imaginations. A good worship space is not merely the result of decor; it is also the product of mature theological reflection about the nature of worship. Form follows function, and well-planned sanctuaries communicate by their very design the kind of worship that takes place within.

TENT, TEMPLE, AND TABLE

Over the centuries, Christians have found it possible to transform almost any kind of space into a place of worship. Christians have worshiped not only in churches but on battlefields and in brush arbors, in funeral homes and movie theaters, in warehouses and skating rinks. However, the Christian community rarely leaves a place unchanged. When an artist opens a studio in an abandoned train depot, suddenly the place blossoms with canvases, palettes, and other signs that something new is happening in this place. Just so, when a congregation worships in a space, unmistakable signs announce that this is now a place of worship. A candle is lit, an altar is set, a Bible is opened, a cross is placed on a table: something symbolic is done to establish that, at least for a few moments, this place—whether it be a clearing in the woods, a stretch of sand on the beach, or a school auditorium—is a place of holy meeting, a place of worship.

But the setting up of a worship space, whether a temporary altar or a more permanent church building, is a complex matter. Christians want the arrangement of worship space to communicate not only *that* worship happens here but also *what kind* of worship takes place. If one church has an amphitheater-style auditorium with a sloping floor and hundreds of padded, spring-loaded seats all facing a mammoth projection screen, and another church has a plain, unadorned room with folding chairs arranged in a circle around a simple wooden table, these are not just different buildings;

they represent radically different understandings of the faith. A worship space is a physical expression of what the worshipers here believe about the nature of God and the character of faith.

Several years ago, when a congregation in the South built a new church building, decision-makers choose not to build the usual steeple-and-columns neo-colonial design typical of many other churches in their area. Instead, they asked their architect to design something a bit more daring and contemporary, a bold structure with natural stone, unexpected angles, and a dramatic use of glass. The result? Some love it and others hate it, but among the critics the most common complaint is, "Why, it doesn't even look like a church!"

What does a church look like? Is there a pattern, a template, a set of universal standards? At one level, of course not. Churches can and should come in many flavors architecturally. The storefront church jammed in next to the adult bookstore looks every bit as much like a church as St. Patrick's Cathedral in New York. At another level, though, we can say that a church ought to look like a church, and what we mean here has less to do with architectural style and everything to do with function. A church building should not say, "Look at this building; this is the church," but instead, "Come inside this building to *be* the church; enter this place to *act* as the church." This means, according to worship professors James White and Susan White, that the focal point of a Christian church is always on the inside, where the people gather and the action of worship is done, not on the outside, "as in a pagan temple built as a monument to a god, where the people are excluded from the interior."[3] They note that "the façades of many great churches were left unfinished for centuries," since the exterior mattered little compared to the worship space inside.[4]

In this regard, the Bible provides some excellent clues as to what the inside of a church should look like. There are no blueprints in Scripture, of course, but there are at least three biblical models of places of worship—the tent, the temple, and the house (with a table)[5]—and each one captures something essential about the nature of worship. These models disclose dynamics of worship that every good worship space should seek to express, and as such, they can serve as navigational guides in deciding which direction to go in designing a worship space. They are the tent, the temple, and the house (with table).

The Tent

During the wilderness period, the Israelites, it is said, worshiped in a tent, a tabernacle, a moveable sanctuary. As described in Exodus 25–30, this tabernacle was huge, the size of a circus tent, and its design and furnishings were reminiscent of the temple in Jerusalem, which was built many years later. In fact, many biblical scholars wonder whether images of the Jerusalem temple have been imported retrospectively into the memories of the tabernacle, since they find it difficult to imagine this enormous tent and its lavish appointments being carted around the desert by nomadic tribes. It is more likely, these scholars say, that the biblical picture of the tabernacle is a product of theological imagination and that in the desert days Israel's worship was housed in smaller and simpler tents (the sort of dwelling implied in Exodus 33:7).

Perhaps so, but in this case the theological point trumps the historical data. The biblical writers wanted to show that Israel traveled through the wilderness worshiping in a movable temple. The sanctuary traveled with them, because God traveled with them, too. These writers were aware that the transition to a permanent place of worship, however inevitable and desirable that may have been, also involved some loss. A God who is on the move with the people cannot be easily domesticated or relegated to one static location. When King David, newly settled in his cedar palace, frets that his house is nicer than God's tent and resolves to build a permanent sanctuary, God declines the honor: "I have not lived in a house since the day I brought up the people of Israel from Egypt to this day, but I have been moving about in a tent and a tabernacle" (2 Sam. 7:6).

If a worship space is to preserve the memory of the tabernacle, it should allow for movement within worship, should convey the truth that God's people are constantly on foot serving God in the world, and should communicate that the place of worship is not a cul-de-sac but a way station for pilgrims on the move.

Temple

From the tenth century B.C. forward, Israel's worship moved from the animal skins of the tent to the stones of the temple. Three temples were built in all, each one on the same site, Mount Zion in Jerusalem. If the portability of the tabernacle taught Israel that God was on the move through time and circumstance, the majesty of the temple taught Israel that God was an awesome and holy presence. Sirach provides a dramatic description of temple worship around 200 B.C., stating that the priest, who wore a glorious robe, received an offering of wine from the attendants and then poured it out at the foot of the altar. Trumpets sounded, and

> Then all the people together quickly
> > fell to the ground on their faces to worship their Lord,
> > the Almighty, God Most High.
> Then the singers praised him with their voices
> > in sweet and full-toned melody.
> And the people of the Lord Most High offered
> > their prayer before the Merciful One,
> until the order of worship of the Lord was ended,
> > and they completed his ritual.
>
> (Sirach 50:17-19)

The temple, then, is a place of awe and sacrifice, mystery and devotion, and if a worship space is to preserve the memory of the temple, it should communicate wonder and the transcendence of God, prompting worshipers to bow before the presence of the Holy One.

The House

When the third temple was destroyed by the Romans in A.D. 70, the focus of Jewish worship shifted to synagogues, houses of prayer and learning. Some of the earliest Christians worshiped in the temple (Luke 24:50), but they also worshiped in the synagogues, and then finally took the essence of synagogue worship into their own homes.

To worship in a house, whether it be the synagogue or a domestic dwelling, shifts the emphasis of worship to the gathered assembly and to the instruction, conversation, interaction, and fellowship that takes place among the participants. Especially for the early Christians, house worship afforded the opportunity to gather at the table for the breaking of bread. All places of worship embody ideas of holiness, and if the tent conveyed God's holiness as a presence moving through history, and the temple conveyed God's holiness as reigning mercifully and majestically over all creation, then the house communicates the holiness of God's people, the body of Christ. If the tent says, "Follow me," and the temple says, "Take off your shoes for you are on holy ground," then the house says, "You are a chosen race, a royal priesthood, a holy nation, God's own people."

If a worship space is to preserve the memory of house worship, it should provide space for the gathering of the people and support their inter-action, mutual participation, and communion.

From the tent, then, we receive the idea of movement in worship; and from the temple, the idea of awe; and from the house, the idea of *koinonia*, fellowship. Let us now explore how these three worship impulses can find tangible expression in a congregation's worship space.

PUTTING IT TOGETHER IN THE HOUSE OF GOD

For most of us, a church sanctuary is a simply a room where worship takes place. It is either large or small, beautiful or not, plain or ornate, traditional or contemporary. However, in their fine book on church architecture, James White and Susan White enable us to put on a new set of spectacles and to see a sanctuary in a somewhat different way. They picture a sanctuary as a collection of seven different spaces in which worship actions take place: gathering space, movement space, congregational space, choir space, altar-table space, baptismal space, and pulpit-lectern space.[6] They are quick to say that "all the parts of a building are interrelated" and that "the sum is much more than just a total of isolated parts," but by parsing a worship space into these discrete areas they allow us to think more clearly about how a building can support effective worship and how the movement of the tent, the awe of the temple, and the community of the house and table can all be achieved in a single room. Let us explore how the vital churches made use of these spaces:

1. Gathering Space

Symbolically, the people of God stream to the place of worship from their many places of ministry in the world. Logistically and practically, however, they come to the sanctuary from many locations—places like the parking lot, the education building, the fellowship hall, the choir robing room, the coffeepot, and the restrooms. So, viewing the gathering for worship both as a theological image and as a more practical matter of traffic flow, a church needs a place into which the congregation can merge from many directions.

We have already noted in chapter 3 how many churches today are providing larger, well-lit, and comfortably furnished narthexes, or foyers, for gathering. The vital churches, for the most part, are part of this trend. Some of them have expanded the size of their welcoming space outside the sanctuary (or have changed the floor plan and pattern of foot traffic to allow for a side room to serve as a narthex), made the entrance to the church easily accessible for wheelchairs, have opened up as many doors as possible into this gathering spot, and have made sure that the paths to this entering point for worship are well-marked.

To make the gathering place one of warmth, accessibility, and hospitality fulfills the "house" function of worship, but the vital churches do more than this. They also emphasize the "tent" function of worship by making it clear that the gathering place is not a park but a gateway, not a place to stop but a place to continue on the journey. In part, this is achieved by the appointments of the gathering place, and these are simple things. For example, some of the vital churches have bulletin boards with sign-up sheets and notices of mission, education, and service. Others have photographs and paintings of places where congregational mission takes place. Others have historical artifacts and documents from the congregation's past, as if to say, "We have traveled from there to here, and we are still on the pilgrim road."

The movement aspect of the gathering place is also conveyed by the arrangement of the room. There may be many ways to enter the room, but everything about the placement of the furnishings invites a flow toward the place of worship. "We have come individually from everywhere," the room seems to say, "but we are going together in there to worship." The room heightens the anticipation and expectation of worship.

2. Movement Space

One of the inherent problems with many older church buildings is a lack of movement space (areas visible to the whole congregation, in the center of things, where movement and active elements of worship can occur, such as people gathering in groups for prayer, ceremonies of recognition and dedication, liturgical dance, or the playing of musical instruments). The pews and other furnishings typically fill all of the usable floor space, so there is room for the congregation to sit and room for the ministerial leaders to stand, but not much else.

All of the vital congregations, however, managed to provide for movement space. Such movement clearly picks up on the "tent" theme of worship, but depending upon the activity involved, the "temple" and "house" functions can also be present. How did these churches find the space? One of the vital churches, which has a newer building, had designed the sanctuary to provide for movement, but the other vital churches had removed pews and rearranged chancel furniture to create such places.

A pastor of one of the vital churches, as soon as he arrived as the new minister, knew two things about worship: first, the sanctuary desperately needed movement space and, second, the rearrangement of furnishings necessary to provide it would be controversial. So this pastor, believing that he could seek forgiveness easier than he could get permission, asked the sexton to meet him at the church in the dead of night one Saturday, and the two of them unbolted the front row of pews and hid them in a storeroom. When the congregation arrived for worship the next day, everyone could sense that the sanctuary was different, but no one could put a finger on exactly *what* was different. All they knew was that the room looked larger, more inviting, and since no one sat in the front pews anyway, no one was displaced from a customary seat. The pastor made a point of conducting much of the service—the prayers, the cares and concerns, the welcoming of new members—from this new open space. For the offertory anthem, a chamber music group set up its music stands in the space, and during the children's sermon the kids seemed much more comfortable and attentive when assembled in this space. After several weeks, the pastor "confessed" from the pulpit what he had done and asked if anyone would like to see the missing pews replaced. Not a soul did.

3. Congregational Space

The vital congregations did what they could to enable the congregational space to emphasize the "house" dimension of worship, the gathering together of the assembly. For those congregations with movable seating, this meant creating a semicircular arrangement for the chairs. For those churches with traditional fixed-pew seating, two measures were taken. First, ushers roped off the rear pews, making sure that people sat in comfortably full pews, beginning at or near the front. This gave a sense of being in a gathered community, related to each other, which is an experience far to be prized over a scattered congregation sitting in isolated little clusters in pet pews. Second, the lighting was set up so that the congregational space nearest to the front was bathed in a warm and cheerful circle of light. This creation of a ring of light around the central action of worship was especially important in the larger, more shadowy, cathedral-type buildings.

Not everything about the arrangement of congregational space is aimed at the "house" aspect of worship. Even those churches with seating in the semi-round took care to ensure that the chairs were tilted somewhat toward the chancel and not just aimed at each other. This conveyed the conviction, bound up in the "temple" image, that a community had gathered ultimately to encounter a reality beyond itself and not merely for communal encounters.

Moreover, while it is not unusual for a church to have altar hangings and other symbols in the chancel area, several of the vital congregations were very sensitive to the power of color and visuals in the congregational area as well, placing banners, posters, and other objects of art there. On Pentecost Sunday, for example, one of the vital churches had taken large bolts of brilliant red cloth and hung a flowing swatch in a wave pattern down each side wall the full length of the sanctuary. A dozen or more bare-limbed trees had been placed throughout the room, and every branch had been festooned with red and orange carnations. A huge spray of red roses lay at the foot of the communion table, and across the facing of the balcony a gnarled grapevine was strung, it, too, filled with red and orange flowers. In short, the whole room was ablaze with vivid color and the sensation of movement; everywhere one looked there was Pentecostal fire.

4. Choir Space

Most of the vital churches worked hard architecturally to underscore the dual function of the choir—that choir members are both worship leaders and members of the assembly. On the one hand, to place the choir front and center can turn them from leaders of the whole congregation into performers of sacred music. Moreover, this arrangement makes it virtually impossible for the choir to be perceived or to function as members of the gathered congregation. On the other hand, to place the choir in the back or in a balcony loft, out of sight, can be an overcompensation. Because they cannot be easily seen, this location reduces their ability to serve as worship leaders.

The ideal is to place the choir in a "borderline" position—that is, in a spot that places them among the worshiping congregation and allows their music to come from the gathered assembly but also in a spot that allows them to be seen and heard easily so that they can exercise musical leadership. Finding this "borderline" spot usually requires some ingenuity and willingness to compromise. Some of the vital congregations placed the choir in the front-most section of the congregation; others placed them so that they completed the circle of a congregation in the round. Another, whose choir was a mariachi band, positioned the musicians in the side apse. Still others, by virtue of older architecture, were forced to house the singers in a choir loft, but planned worship so that the choir could come into the movement space, where they were more a part of the gathered congregation but could still be seen and heard, for special music.

5. Altar-Table Space,
6. Baptismal Space,
7. Pulpit-Lectern Space

Most of the vital churches had, whenever possible, moved these crucial worship spaces—the altar-table, the baptismal furnishings, and the pulpit-lectern—closer to the congregational space. The goal seemed to be to get these spaces closer to the people for a very practical reason, so that communion, baptism, and preaching could be seen and heard clearly, and also for a theological reason, to symbolize the truth that worship involves the community gathering around these events.

It is important to note, however, that even though these three spaces were often brought nearer to the assembly, the spaces remained separate and were never conflated or confused with the congregational space. One of the typical mistakes made by congregations trying to make their worship more "contemporary" is, in the name of intimacy and casual worship, to turn all worship space into congregational space. For example, the preacher will not speak from a pulpit or from a place in the chancel, but rather will wander up and down the aisles and around the whole sanctuary during the sermon. Or a table or baptismal bowl will be brought out of a storeroom when needed but not given a permanent place in the sanctuary. The vital congregations, however, retained an important distance and separation, as well as a proximity. This decision preserved the "temple" dimension of worship, a sense of mystery and awe. Although much of the worship service in some of the vital churches is conducted in the movement space, in the midst, as it were, of the people, it is significant that in no case did any of the preachers abandon the symbolism of the pulpit to wander out in the congregational space as they preached. The pulpit was close to the people, but it also represented a word of grace coming from beyond the assembly, coming from God. Also, even in those of the vital congregations where worship is more informal, churches that tend to set the Lord's table right in the middle of the congregation, there was still communicated—through words and actions of reverence—an understanding that the table was something to be approached with awe.

HUMILITY AND EXCITEMENT IN STONE

"Christian worship does change," write James White and Susan White, "and therefore church architecture must change. . . . No one [in the 1950s] contemplated banners, large baptismal fonts, or moveable seating. A more humble architecture . . . would have served us better."[7] Indeed, one way to sum up much that the vital congregations have done with their buildings is that they have made them more humble, not more lavish. They have opened up the doors on the gathering space and made the congregational space more hospitable. They have cleared out space for the people and brought the signs of God's presence nearer to the assembly. But in doing so, they have also renewed a sense of excitement, color, art, and movement in worship. The space of worship vibrates with the potential of an encounter between God and humanity, an engagement that will break out in song and movement, praise and devotion, surrender and service.

CHAPTER 7

Serving in This Place: Neighborhoods and Mission

S ome time ago I spent several days working with a local congregation—teaching, preaching, meeting with the staff, talking with the officers and other members. When my time with them had come to an end, a few members of the congregation, all very active in various programs of the church, took me to the airport. On the way one of them asked me, "So what do you think of our church?"

I replied with the usual courtesies. "I thoroughly enjoyed myself. The congregation made me feel right at home. I was glad to be here." This was all true, even though something about this congregation had bothered me. I just couldn't put my finger on precisely what it was.

A woman then said, "No, really; some of us have been worried about our church lately. What did you honestly think of it?"

The car was quiet with expectation, and I could tell this was an invitation for candor, so I took it. "I did enjoy your church," I replied, "but truthfully something about it troubles me. I just can't bring it into focus. All the obvious signs are positive. The church is growing a little; the staff seems quite able; attendance at worship is pretty good; there don't seem to be any major conflicts. It's just that, I don't know. . . ."

"It's just that there is no energy," a man in the group said. "The pieces are all in place, but there's no passion. Worship feels blah." The others nodded agreement.

The key turned in the lock. "That's what I was feeling," I responded. "You've named it. People in your church seem happy enough; nobody's throwing punches in committee meetings, but it seems more like a puddle of contentment than a flow of energy. There is no direction to congregational life, no excitement about what you're doing."

What was dawning on me was that I had been with this congregation for several days and had participated in many phases of its life, but I still had no clear idea what this congregation was about, what it was in the world to do. If it had been a shop, I would not have known what they were selling; if it had been a restaurant, I could not have described its cuisine. On the surface, it was a good congregation, but I could not discern its mission. "You are the salt of the earth, but if the salt has lost its savor . . . ?"

To be sure, congregations are complex organizations, and they can almost never be narrowed to a single focus, nor should we try. Even so, if one hangs around a healthy congregation for very long, it soon becomes clear what is serving as its organizing center, where its passions and central commitments lie. For one congregation it may be evangelism, for another education, for still another ministry with the disadvantaged or providing fellowship and mutual compassion for families. But sound congregations are about something; they have missional themes that generate enthusiasm and stimulate involvement. The problem with the congregation I had just visited was that it was all dressed up with nowhere to go.

In the vital congregations, by contrast, there is a clear congregational mission, a vibrant energy center of action and service that gives the congregation its particular identity, and the impact of this mission is felt in every dimension of its life, including worship. Thus, another of the marks of the vital and faithful congregations can be stated as follows:

> CHARACTERISTIC 6.
> VITAL AND FAITHFUL CONGREGATIONS
> HAVE A STRONG CONNECTION
> BETWEEN WORSHIP AND LOCAL MISSION,
> AND THIS CONNECTION IS EXPRESSED
> IN EVERY ASPECT OF THE WORSHIP SERVICE.

A good way to glimpse how a church's mission shapes its overall identity is to try this experiment: think of five or six congregations that you know fairly well, and try to describe each of them in a single sentence. You may come up with thumbnail descriptions like: "St. Andrew's has a very active soup kitchen and a homeless shelter," or "Faith Church has a new family-life center and a recreational ministry to families," or "Central Church has a deep commitment to the downtown business community," or "Morris Avenue Church really draws in the youth and young adults," or "Macedonia Church has a strong refugee-placement program," or "Trinity Church has a superb music program and a great preaching tradition." Now there is obviously much more going on in each of these congregations than your snapshots capture, but where did you get these impressions? Churches develop reputations—theologically, programmatically, and missionally—because they channel their resources in this or that direction, and insofar as these reputations are accurate they represent decisions these congregations have made about how they will spend their money, time, and energy.

Two cautions here. First, we should reiterate the truth that healthy congregations have focused commitments and clear missional themes. But this does not mean that they are one-cause churches or that the spectrum of their congregational life can be compressed to a single band. A few years back, to gain a few yards in the fast-food scrimmage, Kentucky Fried Chicken built an ad campaign around the slogan "We do one thing well. We do chicken right." This implied, of course, that in contrast to the burger joints that foolishly try to do it all—burgers, fish, ribs, chicken, and roast beef—and end up being mediocre at everything, KFC had found its niche, targeted its fast-food mission, and thereby achieved excellence. Congregations, however, are not like KFC. A sharply defined missional identity does not slim down the range of ministries and programs; rather it supplies direction and coherence to the full orb of congregational activities.

Consider the example of "First Church," a very active congregation in the downtown of a midsize midwestern city. Forty years ago a cluster of strong congregations was located in the center city. But as the people, the housing, and the money drifted out to the suburbs, so gradually did the churches. One by one, the downtown congregations bought property in the outlying areas until only First Church was left downtown. The leaders of First Church considered moving as well, even scanned the real-estate market for suitable sites, but they finally decided that the inner city needed a Christian witness and made the deliberate choice to stay downtown.

If one observes First Church from a distance, it looks much like every other congregation of comparable size. It has a staff, a schedule of weekly worship services, a Christian education program, midweek Bible studies, monthly family night suppers, a youth ministry, and an array of social ministries such as a clothes closet, a food pantry, after-school tutoring, and a literacy program. Draw closer, however, and it becomes clear that every phase of First Church's life has been shaped by the decision to be a witness downtown. A minister to the community is on staff; the prayers and hymns and sermons in worship reflect the church's mission to the city; the church school often features courses on urban issues; the youth help stock and staff the clothes closet and the food pantry; the family-night suppers include street persons as regulars; and one of the Bible studies is held on Thursdays at 7 A.M. and features a continental breakfast to serve the folk who work downtown. In sum, it is quite clear what First Church is about—to be a light in the center city—but the life of First Church is far more complex than "we do one thing well." It does a hundred things, and a lot of them are done very well, but everything it does is shaped by and comes to focus in its primary mission.

The second caution is that, while healthy congregations may have a clearly focused missional identity, that does not mean that everybody in the congregation would use the same language to describe the mission. Often a congregation's core identity lies at the tacit level. It can be woven so deeply into the fabric of a church's activity that it works quietly in the background, out of sight but still shaping the congregation—what Christian educators sometime call the "implied curriculum" of a congregation's life.

Consider the case of "Sardis Church," a remarkable congregation situated in one of the poorer neighborhoods of a large city. In a society where most congregations are segregated by race and class, Sardis is a diverse and integrated congregation of poor and wealthy; black, white, brown, and yellow; people from many cultures and conditions. Its central mission is to be "a house of prayer for all people," and it has made hospitality, reconciliation, inclusivity, and mutual understanding its primary focus. The congregation works hard at this mission, and whoever comes to the door of Sardis Church soon finds a warm welcome and a place in the community. Someone has described Sardis as a kind of "spiritual potluck supper"; everybody brings some gift to the place of worship, and the members of Sardis have a way of naming and receiving those gifts, and then placing each person's gift among the others on the banquet table.

Recently, a team of sociologists of religion, seeking to study "a multicultural, multiethnic, multiclass congregation" latched on to Sardis. What they found was a congregation notably coherent in its practices of hospitality and unity. The way Sardis worships and works together draws people in, creates an ethos of mutual understanding, and allows this diverse group to worship and to serve as one. However, when the researchers pulled aside individual members of Sardis and asked them to describe why Sardis is the way it is, an amazing variety of categories and theological views emerged. Some people at Sardis have theological views that border on fundamentalism, and they believe that life at Sardis enables them to carry out the literal commands of the Bible. Others expressed a broad, liberal humanitarianism, saying, "All people are of equal worth and dignity, and we express this at our church." Still others use the language of psychology, describing Sardis's mission in terms of "self-esteem and growth toward embracing the radically other." In other words, the "implied curriculum" at Sardis shapes a community of prayer and welcome, and the members of Sardis live and work and worship in remarkable harmony. But they talk about this very differently. Sardis's primary mission of unity and hospitality and reconciliation is embodied at the tacit level of practice even though the members do not have a common language to articulate it.

Swinging Saloon Doors

Once upon a time it was popular for churches to put the phrase "Enter to Worship; Depart to Serve" on the cover of their worship bulletins. The idea, of course, was that the congregation comes into the sanctuary for worship and then heads out into the world to do Christian service. However, critics of this phrase quite rightly pointed out that worship and service cannot be so neatly divided. When a congregation prays for the world in worship, that is a form of Christian service, and when a congregation feeds the hungry or cares for the sick or works for justice, these are also worshipful acts of praise.

Figuratively, the doors of a sanctuary ought to swing in and out like saloon doors. If a congregation is praying that people in the community be adequately housed, then it ought to be flowing out the door to build Habitat for Humanity houses. Conversely, if the congregation is building Habitat for Humanity houses, then it should be flowing in the door to pray for and to preach about fair housing.

In the vital congregations, the rhythms and relationships between worship and mission were evident. It is not that every word and phrase of the worship service was mechanically connected to some mission program; it is more that one gained, in the totality of worship, an awareness, at least at the tacit level, of what this congregation does in the world. Imagine gathering in a hospital chapel for a service of daily prayer with a group of physicians and nurses about to begin the day. The language of healing and compassion and discernment would reverberate through the service. Imagine worshiping with a group of United Nations troops about to leave on a dangerous peace-keeping mission. The language of peace and reconciliation and protection in times of danger would abound. Imagine worshiping with volunteers for Bread for the World as they embark on an assignment to persuade Congress to allocate more money for starving children. Would not the language of hunger and feeding, justice and hope fill the prayers? Anyone who worshiped with these groups would soon discover their mission just by praying the prayers, singing the hymns, listening to the preaching.

One of the vital congregations has a strong ministry in a nearby state-run institution for mentally disabled children, many of them with Down's syndrome. Not only do some of the members of the congregation volunteer their time to care for and to teach these children, but they go to the facility on Sunday morning and bring as many of the children as wish to come to worship. There are always several of these children among the congregation, and they are very audible in the singing of the hymns and the other congregational responses. This church observes the Lord's Supper every week, and does so by gathering in a large circle around the communion table, with worshipers holding hands. The minister begins the communion portion of the service by inviting people to the table, reminding them that this table belongs to Christ and that everyone is welcome. The congregation then responds in unison, "Everyone is welcome at this table." The sound of the Down's syndrome children joining in that response is a joyful sound indeed. These children are the focus of congregational mission, but they are also full and regular participants in worship. Thus, it is difficult to tell where worship ends and service begins.

Another of the vital congregations, located in a large urban area, has a ministry to the city's arts community. The church holds Bible studies and prayer groups designed especially for actors, painters, musicians, dancers, sculptors, and other artists. They encourage the use of the church building for neighborhood art shows. As a consequence, the worship of this congregation brims full with artistic expression as the artists who receive from the congregation through the week contribute their talents on Sunday. From the cover of the worship bulletin to the artwork on the wall of the narthex to the music in the service to the seasonal decorations in the sanctuary to the liturgical dance, the relationship between mission and worship can be seen and heard.

Still another of the vital churches understands part of its mission to be serving as a social conscience in its community. Members of this congregation frequently show up at city council sessions, school board meetings, public hearings, and the like to speak up for the poor, the homeless, prisoners, and others who may not have full political voice on their own. The annual Good Friday service in this church is most unusual and is shaped by this mission. The service includes the expected elements: prayers, seasonal hymns, and the reading of the Passion narrative, but most of the service does not take place in the sanctuary. The congregation gathers at the church for an opening hymn and prayer, then they board buses to travel to several locations in their community. They stop at the local jail to read the biblical story of the arrest of Jesus, and then they pray for those in the jail, remembering that Jesus, too, was imprisoned. Then they travel to the courthouse to read of the trial of Jesus, praying for those who, like Jesus, are on trial. Then they travel to the cemetery to read the story of Jesus' death and burial, remembering those who grieve and those who, like Jesus, face their own hour of dying. The great narrative of Good Friday worship is taken into their community, and their community, the setting for their mission, is gathered up into their worship.

EXPANDING THE "MINUTE FOR MISSION"

A regular feature of worship in many congregations is the "Minute for Mission," a time in worship when some program or mission opportunity is described to the congregation. There is, of course, much that is good and right about the "Minute for Mission." Congregations do want to be informed about mission opportunities, and the lay leaders of these various mission projects need to have places in worship to bear witness to their work and to invite congregational support.

But the language betrays us. The very phrase "Minute for Mission" communicates something small and sealed off from the rest of worship, as if someone hit the "pause" button on worship while the church experiences a missional interlude.

The vital congregations have no "minutes for mission." The service they are called to do in the world and that defines their congregational identity is present throughout their worship. It is present in the prayers and the hymns, the preaching and the joys and concerns, because, as we observed in chapter 3, people still want to give themselves away to a great and holy cause. People come to church to join with others in offering themselves and their service to God, and when the offering plates are passed, we put in not only our money but also our mission and our very selves.

CHAPTER 8

Come to the Joyful Dance:
Memory and Celebration

Because I am a seminary professor and not the pastor of a congregation, I sometimes find myself in the role of "visiting minister." The regular minister is on vacation or away for a study leave or ill, and a substitute is needed; so I am called.

When I arrive at the church, I always pull aside the most informed-looking person I can find because I have questions about how this church does its service. Do you announce the hymns? Do you use the Lord's Prayer, and do you say "trespasses," "debts," or "sins"? Do you say "descended into hell" in the Apostles' Creed? Do you have an offertory prayer? Does it come before or after the offering? Does the congregation stand, sit, or kneel for prayer? Is there a benediction? Is it pronounced from the pulpit, the center of the chancel, the rear of the sanctuary?

Practical things like that.

Amazingly, the people I ask hardly ever know for sure. Even if they have worshiped in this church for decades, most of the time they scratch their heads, gaze off into space, and then take a wild guess or sheepishly admit they haven't the foggiest notion about such worship logistics. Though they have experienced worship week in and week out for years, they could not say, really, whether the minister pronounces the benediction from the front, the back, or from a wire harness swinging out over the congregation. (The one exception to this rule is the church organist. Organists have to mind the logistics, and they know.)

It may sound like a bad thing that experienced worshipers cannot crisply remember the routine, but, in fact it is a natural thing and, in its own way, a good thing. The main reason they cannot remember the footwork of worship is not because they are indifferent or inattentive but because worship is a dance we eventually learn by heart. Like a fast typist whose knowledge of the keyboard has long since migrated from the head to the fingers, people know when to stand and when to sit and how to respond in worship as a kind of bodily wisdom deeper than what the mind can fully recall about the sequence of the ritual.

In short, the best worship is done to some degree by heart, as an expression of bodily wisdom and a deep memory of how we are to be in the presence of God. Indeed, one of the marks of the vital and faithful congregations can be stated as follows:

> ## CHARACTERISTIC 7.
> VITAL AND FAITHFUL CONGREGATIONS
> HAVE A RELATIVELY STABLE ORDER OF SERVICE
> AND A SIGNIFICANT REPERTOIRE
> OF WORSHIP ELEMENTS AND RESPONSES
> THAT THE CONGREGATION KNOWS BY HEART.

To say that a congregation knows something by heart is not exactly the same as saying that every person in a congregation knows it by heart. Obviously a group cannot know what the individuals who make up that group do not know, but in any congregation there are people at all levels of knowing and remembering. A child or a visitor or a person with Alzheimer's or a new Christian may not yet know, or may have forgotten, the words to a hymn or a creed or a prayer that is familiar to others, but as these people participate in corporate worship, they share in the group experience of memory. What the group knows by heart becomes stamped on the members' hearts as well.

I will always marvel over the day long ago when the worship leader in our congregation called us to do what we did every week, to "confess our faith using the words of the Apostles' Creed." We all stood and began the holy murmur, "I believe in God the Father Almighty . . ." Almost instantly I became aware of a voice I had not heard before in this context. My then 11-year-old son David was standing beside me and reciting the creed, ". . . maker of heaven and earth. And in Jesus Christ his only Son our Lord. . . ."

This was a moment of parental wonder. Where did my son get this Trinitarian formula? We never explicitly taught David the creed, never sat at the kitchen table with flash cards reading "I believe in God the Father

Almighty." He learned it, of course, by being in worship, by hearing it re-
cited week after week, until that day when memory and maturity and motivation converged and he stood up and joined in the chorus of conviction. By
being in a congregation that knew the creed by heart, David was gradually
given something that he, too, will remember by heart.

FORGETTING ONE'S FEET

For a congregation to be able to worship effectively and by heart, at least
three major factors must be present: a stable order of service, an order that
is dramatically meaningful and suspenseful, and an active memory bank of
congregational responses.

First, the issue of stability. Put simply, congregational worship cannot
gain real power unless the order of worship remains fairly fixed over time.
This may seem counterintuitive, especially for a congregation trying to make
worship more exciting and engaging. Doesn't a pattern of worship repeated
week after week soon become routinized and a recipe for boredom? Isn't it
the "been there, done that" predictability of much worship that makes many
churches so ho-hum? Common sense would tell us that the only way out of
the rut would be an ever-changing order full of fresh turns and fascinating
surprises.

As a matter of fact, though, when it comes to human rituals, the more
powerful they are the less they tend to change. A frothy morning-radio
personality who helps to kill a little time as we commute to work has to
come up with some new shtick every day, but when it comes around to a
wedding or a funeral or a family reunion or the way we observe Christmas,
the familiar and well-worn path is the one we want to travel. The repeated
patterns of these rituals are not like telephone poles whipping past us with
numbing repetitiveness as we speed down the highway; they are instead
like channel markers, guiding us into deep water. Even ancient and powerful rituals do change, of course, but they tend to evolve slowly, adapting
gradually to new circumstances. A congregation that can never change its
pattern of worship is certainly in trouble, but a congregation that can change
its worship every week is in much deeper trouble, because nothing is being
learned by heart. As C. S. Lewis famously observed,

> Novelty, simply as such, can have only an entertainment value.
> And [people] don't go to church to be entertained. They go to *use*

the service, or, if you prefer, to *enact* it. . . . [I]t works best —
when through long familiarity, we don't have to think about it. As
long as you notice, and have to count, the steps, you are not yet
dancing but only learning to dance. . . . The perfect church service
would be one we were almost unaware of; our attention would
have been on God.[1]

If worshipers are to cut loose at the dance, then they need to learn the
steps without counting and without watching their feet. If the order of worship shifts frequently, the congregation may be entertained, may even say
they are delighted by the snappy surprises, but they will also remain in their
seats and stay off the dance floor. Thus, an order of service that remains
fairly stable over time is important for effective worship.

Stability alone, however, is not enough. A stable, reliable pattern can
still make for bad worship because orders of service can be boring, trivial,
or even destructive. This point leads us to the second factor necessary for
people to worship by heart. The order of service needs to be dramatically
meaningful and suspenseful, something worshipers want to put their hearts
into. Worshipers need to learn the dance steps of worship, but there is a
difference between a waltz and the hokey-pokey. The first is fluid, graceful,
full of suspense, spontaneity, and even unpredictable movement, while the
second is largely a matter of mere repetition, something one finally out-
grows. Unfortunately, too many churches do hokey-pokey worship. People
have no trouble mastering the rhythm and the steps—you put your left foot
in, you put your left foot out, you put your left foot in and shake it all about
. . . that's what it's all about—but ultimately, who cares? The body goes
mindlessly through the paces, but thoughts eventually wander.

Authentic worship is more like the waltz. It has a stable order of steps,
but these steps generate movement that has coherence, beauty, and depth
of meaning. We do not need to belabor this point here since it was more
fully discussed in chapter 4, but a good order of worship has action, drama,
and complexity. It is a piece of profound community theater built on the
Gospel narrative, and when the worshipers know their parts by heart they
are drawn more deeply into the event and the meaning of the story. A good
order of worship is also suspenseful, not in the sense that we have no idea
how things are going to turn out in the end, but in the sense that the order of
worship is an unfolding plot moving toward resolution.

Watch Fred Astaire and Ginger Rogers dance in one of those great
classic movies. They obviously know their steps by heart, and neither of

them is counting or watching their feet. Like the best of worshipers, they have practiced and worked and done this a thousand times, and their movements have become fluid, harmonious, and free, seemingly transcending active thought. But, there is more going on here than a pattern of dance steps well executed. Fred Astaire and Ginger Rogers are not the Rockettes or the Marine Marching Band, kicking their legs mechanistically to the rhythm; they are not simply doing calisthenics—one-two, one-two, one-two. They are dancing a narrative, an ancient and ever-fascinating epic of suspenseful romantic attraction, sexual allure, and love. The fact that the movements of the dance have become for them a matter of bodily wisdom enables their minds and spirits to be fully focused on the meaning of what their bodies so gracefully do. Their dance is a great love story, an acted-out drama of courtship and passion. The fact that they know it by heart frees them to be absorbed by this story, with each other, and with the power of the dance itself.

C. S. Lewis is right; the "perfect church service" would be one where we are all like Fred Astaire and Ginger Rogers, gliding around the sanctuary mindless of the steps—hymn, prayer, sermon—because we are absorbed by the great Gospel narrative those steps are telling, our attention fully focused upon God.

The events of worship are not just actions—standing, sitting, bowing, kneeling. They are also words—singing, saying, confessing, preaching—and in the vital churches many of these spoken parts were also known from memory. This was the third major factor in effective worship done by heart: the congregations had a reservoir of prayers, creeds, songs, and responses committed to memory. To be sure, most of the vital churches used hymnals or song sheets and some of them used prayer books, but in none of them was worship dominated by acts of reading material off a page. A significant portion of the words of worship had been committed to memory.

Several summers ago on a trip to Chicago I slipped away one afternoon for a baseball game at Wrigley Field. Just as with a Sunday service, there was the particular program for the day, Cubs versus Astros as I recall, but the specifics of that one baseball game were nested in the framework of the larger repeated ritual: the crowds streaming into the great old ballpark, the umpires and managers meeting at home plate, the singing of the national anthem, the throwing out of the first ball, the pitchers warming up before each inning, the hawkers wandering through the stands selling hotdogs and peanuts, the seventh-inning stretch.

Indeed, as the top of the seventh inning came to a close, a ripple of excitement passed through the stands. Everybody knew what was coming and had been waiting for it with eager anticipation. As the ballfield organist began to play some chords of introduction, the crowd leapt to its feet, and famed Cubs announcer Harry Caray leaned out of the broadcast booth, microphone in hand, bellowing merrily to the crowds, "OK, everybody, ah-one and ah-two. . . . Take me out to the ball game. Take me out with the crowd." As Caray waved his microphone like a conductor's wand, all of us in the crowd were swaying back and forth, singing and loving every word of the familiar song. "Buy me some peanuts and Cracker Jack, I don't care if I never get back." In unison we lifted our hands to the sky, our fingers ticking off the numbers, "For it's one, two, three strikes you're out at the o-o-o-l-d ball game."

We knew the ritual, we knew the motions, we knew the words, we knew the song. Everything was ingrained in our common memory, and it was a great and joyful moment. Imagine how we would have responded if Caray had announced, "Today, instead of 'Take Me Out to the Ball Game,' we'll be singing 'Mockingbird Hill.' Ushers will be passing out song sheets." There would have been a riot on Chicago's Waveland Avenue.

Memories Are Made of This

Part of the joy of worship is to know the motions, know the words, know the song. The vital congregations knew their order of worship and moved through it with deep familiarity. What is more, the worshipers had active roles—speaking, singing, moving—and many of these they could perform from memory. Enabling a congregation to be at this point involves several practical strategies:

1. *Once is not enough.* Some worship planners have the misguided notion that congregational prayers and responses need to be newly fashioned or spontaneously uttered every week. Nothing could be farther from the truth. While there is obviously a place for extemporaneous prayer and improvisation in worship, one-time-use prayers and off-the-top-of-the-head responses often turn out to be forgettable throwaways, language that means something to the person who uses it but that has a hard time gaining any traction with the whole congregation. Worship leaders can and should

create new prayers and responses, but if they are carefully constructed and have strong metaphors and images (whether written or oral), they deserve to be used for several weeks or more in order to fulfill their promise. A finely crafted prayer or a thoughtfully created response grows in power the more a congregation becomes acquainted with it and uses it. Take, for example, the following well-known prayer attributed to St. Francis of Assisi:

Lord, make me an instrument of your peace.
Where there is hatred, let me sow love;
where there is injury, pardon;
where there is doubt, faith;
where there is despair, hope;
where there is darkness, light;
where there is sadness, joy;

O divine Master, grant that I may not so much seek
to be consoled, as to console,
to be understood, as to understand,
to be loved, as to love.
For it is in giving that we receive;
it is in pardoning that we are pardoned;
and it is in dying that we are born to eternal life.[2]

This prayer was once new, of course, and it has kept its freshness and power over the centuries because it is not only a beautiful prayer but it also has strong language, rhythmic phrases, and welcoming metaphors and images. Like a wide and generous tree where many birds nest, it has ample places for all manners of experiences and emotions to reside. Every time we pray this prayer, we not only deepen those petitions we have prayed before, but new connections between our lives and the language of the prayer are made. Every time we repeat this prayer, we are less dependent upon the words on the page and more free to pray it by heart. In short, it will mean even more to us the tenth time we pray this prayer than it did the first or the second time.

2. *Bulletins are mainly for visitors.* When the A. B. Dick mimeograph machine entered church life, it meant both good news and bad news for worship. The good news was that the mimeograph machine

(since replaced by the computer, printer, and photocopier) allowed a bulletin or program to be manufactured for every service, enabling each worshiper to have in hand the order of worship, the names and numbers of the hymns, and the weekly parish announcements, and other helpful information. The bad news is that a printed bulletin or program tended to move worship toward weekly novelty and, thus, closer to an experience of reading. The printed bulletin allows us (or perhaps we should say, compels us) to fashion newly written elements of worship for every service. The result is that many congregations spend a significant amount of time in worship reading from the printed page and checking the bulletin to see what comes next.

In the vital congregations, the bulletins were mainly for visitors, and they were crafted as such. They explained things for people encountering them potentially for the first time, like putting beside the word "Doxology" the defining phrase "a song of praise" or printing the full text of the Lord's Prayer or giving a three-sentence description what happens in the observance of the Lord's Supper. These bulletins were expressions of hospitality, guides to newcomers unfamiliar with the words and actions of worship, maps for travelers venturing into a new and strange land.

Vital congregations provided clear and helpful bulletins (or worship programs) for those who needed them, but the goal was to wean regular worshipers away from the bulletin. For worship elements that required responses, such as litanies, the congregational parts were most often easily memorized refrains such as "Lord, hear our prayer" or "Grant us your peace, O God."

You may recall the description in chapter 7 of one of the vital congregations where the Eucharist is observed by gathering the congregation in a large circle around the perimeter of the sanctuary, everyone holding hands and, in effect, surrounding the table. The circle includes young and old, men and women, boys and girls, people of many ethnic groups, children with Down's syndrome, and folk in wheelchairs. The minister welcomes the congregation to the table, always concluding with these words: "All are welcome at Christ's table," to which the congregation responds by heart, "*Everyone* is welcome at Christ's table." This response is printed in the bulletin for the benefit of newcomers, but this response is quickly learned and the bulletins can soon be left in the chairs. Reading from a page is one thing, but to join in with this diverse group of worshipers and to say by heart, "Everyone is welcome at Christ's table," is quite another experience.

The Jesuit scholar Walter Ong claims that the spoken word has a much greater power to form community than does the written word. When someone speaks to a gathering of others, the sound of the voice comes from deep within the speaker and it is heard simultaneously by the whole group. The result is that the interior life of the speaker is manifested and received by others, helping to solidify the group. But suppose, says Ong, that the speaker suddenly distributes a handout and asks everyone to read it. What immediately happens, he maintains, is that "each reader enters into his or her own private reading world, the unity of the audience is shattered, to be reestablished only when oral speech begins again."[3] The same is true when worshipers suddenly start reading their bulletins. The sense of a congregation worshiping in common is violated.

Even in those liturgical traditions whose worship is strongly rooted in a prayer book, the goal is to move from literacy to orality, not to read from the book but to learn the words by heart. Stop a lifelong Episcopalian on the street and say, "Almighty God, unto whom all hearts are open . . . ," and the chances are good that he or she will finish the rest by heart: ". . . all desires known, and from whom no secrets are hid: cleanse the thoughts of our hearts by the inspiration of thy Holy Spirit, that we may perfectly love thee and worthily magnify thy holy name; through Christ our Lord. Amen." When prayers and other elements of worship move from the page to the memory, they gain the capacity to gather experiences unto themselves and to become expressions of a full and rich devotion.

3. *Practice, practice, practice.* It takes concerted effort to teach the elements of worship to a congregation, and in many ways, as we implied in item 1, the best school for worship is worship itself. Using strong prayers and other elements repeatedly in the order of service, to reenact them week after week, allows them to register in the memory banks of the worshipers.

To this on-the-job training that happens in worship itself, some of the vital congregations add more focused forms of worship education. Some take a few minutes before the worship service begins to rehearse a new hymn or the psalm for the day with the congregation, or to point out the images and expressions of a new prayer of confession, or to practice singing a new response. Some others offer complete course on worship, and still others include as a part of their new-member classes what amounts to practice sessions for the event of worship. They go over the order, familiarize people with the hymnal and the other tools of worship, and learn some of the sung and spoken responses.

As any good piano teacher will tell us, all it takes to play the music of the angels is "practice, practice, practice."

On the Way to a Festival

Worship begins with a voice, a cry, a holy summons. God breaks into the mundane routines and cycles of everyday life with a trumpet call to worship: "A voice cries out: 'In the wilderness prepare the way of the Lord, make straight in the desert a highway for our God'" (Isa. 40:3).

That is how worship begins, but where does it go, where does it end? In the wilderness of our lives, a highway is carved, a hand points down the road toward the horizon, but where does the road lead? If a service of worship is traveling God's pilgrim highway, the road takes us to a destination. If worship is a built upon a narrative, the story has a denouement. If worship is a dance, it moves in some direction. But what direction, what ending, what place of pilgrim rest and safe lodging?

Down through the centuries, the classic pattern of Christian worship has taken the worshipers to a place of joyous feasting and song. The basic structure of service most often employed by the church over the generations moves from a time of gathering to the hearing of the Word to the festival table of the Lord's Supper, Holy Communion, the Eucharist. The voice that begins, "In the wilderness prepare the way of the Lord" eventually leads us to the place where it promises, "Ho, everyone who thirsts, come to the waters; and you that have no money, come buy and eat! Come, buy wine and milk without money and without price. . . . For you shall go out in joy and be led back in peace; the mountains and the hills before you shall burst into song, and all the trees of the field shall clap their hands" (Isa. 55:1, 12).

In his book *Planning Blended Worship*, Robert Webber encourages congregations, no matter what denomination, to follow the historically established fourfold worship structure: Gathering, Word, Thanksgiving, Dismissal. Why? Because the fourfold pattern moves from here to there; it goes somewhere. "The fourfold pattern of worship," Webber claims, "is characterized by a narrative quality because it is taking us someplace (the throne room of God's kingdom)"[4] Where is takes us, symbolically, is to heaven, to the great banquet table of God where we feast in communion with the saints and the heavenly hosts. And then the blessing is pronounced and we are sent out to love and serve the Lord.[5]

One of the marks of the vital churches was that they allowed their worship to be governed by this movement toward joyous feasting:

> ### CHARACTERISTIC 8.
> THE VITAL AND FAITHFUL CONGREGATIONS
> MOVE TO A JOYOUS FESTIVAL EXPERIENCE
> TOWARD THE END OF THEIR WORSHIP SERVICES.

How did these congregations move toward a place of joy and thanksgiving in their worship? By several means:

1. Most, but certainly not all, of the vital congregations included the Lord's Supper as regular part of their Sunday worship. In every case, these congregations did not allow the somber and meditative aspects of the Eucharist to be the only theological notes struck, they allowed it also to be a lively celebration. In addition to incorporating quiet and reflective moments and themes, these congregations employ the language and the mood of joy to emphasize that the Eucharist is a thankful heavenly banquet. The music played and sung included not only soft and somber selections but also bright, upbeat, and joyful pieces. The congregations did not sit in the pews passively to receive the elements; there was always congregational movement, either gathering around the table, or coming forward to receive the bread and wine, or standing in clusters as the elements were brought to them.

2. In some of these churches, the preacher for the day started the movement toward joyous festival by the internal development of the sermon. These sermons gradually built toward an emotional climax that led the hearers nearer to the place of festival. Henry Mitchell, well-known teacher of preaching and the founder of the Ecumenical Center for Black Church Studies in Los Angeles, has argued that the move toward celebration in worship should always be initiated by the sermon, which ought, in his view, to end not with a question or a criticism but with a glad affirmation of the Gospel. "Authentic Gospel feasting begets its own irresistible celebration," he writes. "A sermon to the whole person demands a celebration that speaks to and through the emotive, bathing the Word in firm certitude and great, unforgettable rejoicing."[6]

3. Others among the vital congregations made sure that the latter half of the service of worship was filled with joyful elements—music, dance, testimony. This was a time when choirs and soloists and people who simply

stood up in their places in the congregation offered emotionally uplifting music and song. This was a time when heartfelt thanksgivings were spoken by the congregation. It was here in the service that people came forward to speak of blessings and joys in their own faith pilgrimage. It was here in one of the vital congregations that an extraordinarily well-trained, talented, and professional liturgical dance team practically lifted the worshipers out of their seats by dancing with moving emotional power to a spiritual. It was here that the worshipers in the vital congregations heard the sounds of tambourines and drums, guitars and brass, violins and cellos, organs and banjos. Anybody passing by outside these churches during the last part of Sunday worship would, like the older brother in Jesus' parable, have heard the unmistakable sounds of music and dancing and feasting coming from inside the house. Why is this so? Because the good news has been proclaimed, the dead have come to life, the lost have been found, and, as the father of the prodigal son put it, "We had to celebrate and rejoice."

In his majestic book *Iberia*, American novelist James Michener describes the long and dangerous pilgrim road that once led through France and across Spain to the great Cathedral of Santiago de Compostela. For centuries this old road was traveled by many pilgrims of all sorts—kings and queens doing penance, common folk seeking deeper faith, criminals sentenced to make the pilgrimage, priests and nuns renewing their vows, lost souls and seekers of many conditions. As each group of pilgrims drew nearer and nearer to their destination, they would begin to search the horizon, straining to see the enormous cathedral in the distance, hoping for a first glimpse of their long-sought goal. At last one among them would see, ever so faintly, the towers of the great building. When he did, he knew what to do, for there was a much-honored custom among these pilgrim bands. He would turn with excitement to his fellow travelers and exclaim, "My joy!"

So it is with the vital congregations. Moving along the pilgrim way in worship, they eventually arrive at the place where they can glimpse their destination, and nothing can hold back the celebration.

CHAPTER 9

In the Spirit on the Lord's Day: Leadership

"Anne and I are thinking about leaving Central Methodist," said a man to his neighbor over the backyard fence. "I don't know; we've just never been able to warm up to our new pastor. I think we'll try Reverend Bill Maynard's church. One of the guys at work goes there and says he's wonderful, very dynamic."

This is precisely the sort of remark that makes theologians of worship cranky. And well it should. The Reverend Bill Maynard's church? Never been able to warm up to our new pastor? He's wonderful, very dynamic? The idea that a congregation is defined by the personality of its pastor or that people would shop for a church based on the popular appeal of the clergy flies in the face of much that Christian theologians want to affirm about the church and its leadership. Theologically speaking, the Christian church gathers around the presence of God in Christ, not Pastor Maynard or any other human being. What is more, the role of the clergy in a Christian community is to serve, to enable the congregation as a whole to exercise its discipleship, not to form a white-hot personality center to which others gravitate. The fact that congregations build up membership by showcasing their pastors' winning personalities on Sunday morning or by putting their ministers on television in an attempt to make them celebrities is one of the worst features of church life in our society.

However, the protests of theologians aside, the raw truth of the matter is that the personality and gifts of pastoral leadership do matter. They matter to the quality of congregational life, to the attractiveness of the church to visitors, and to the total ethos of worship. Like it or not, the personal style of leadership in a service of worship is a major factor in the effectiveness of that worship. I confess that I wince when I read Kennon L. Callahan's statement, "Warm, winsome pastors communicate a sense of confidence and assurance, grace and encouragement, joy and hope."[1] Was John the Baptist "warm and winsome"? Was Paul? But I find it difficult to argue with the evidence that when a pastor is a strong and attractive presence, the church and its worship often come alive. Callahan is right; the personality of the worship leader is contagious in the congregation, and, for good or ill, the worship leader's presence and style set the tone for worship. Indeed, another mark of the vital and faithful congregations is this:

CHARACTERISTIC 9.

THE VITAL AND FAITHFUL CONGREGATIONS ALL HAVE STRONG, CHARISMATIC PASTORS AS WORSHIP LEADERS.

Is it possible to thread the needle here? Can we find a way honestly to look the facts in the face without doing violence to the theological integrity of worship? Can we account for the power in worship of the leader's personality and style while not, at the same time, playing into the personality-centered, celebrity-dazzled aspects of our culture?

I think so, and the place to begin in thinking about this is, oddly enough, with the World Council of Churches document *Baptism, Eucharist, and Ministry*,[2] or *BEM* as it is often called. First issued in 1982, *BEM* was the product of decades of conversation among Christians around the world, and it was seen as a major breakthrough in ecumenical thought. More than 100 theologians, representing almost every major Christian communion, unanimously recommended *BEM* to the churches for study. For the first time, Christians of the Orthodox, Roman Catholic, Lutheran, Reformed, Methodist, Baptist, Adventist, Pentecostal, and other traditions had found a common language to speak about the crucial, difficult, and often divisive issues of baptism, eucharist, and ministry.

The "Ministry" section of *BEM*, which addresses the role of the ordained clergy among the congregation, was, by all accounts, the most difficult to construct. At one level it may seem strange that Christians found it easier to agree about the thorny doctrines of baptism and eucharist than they did about the nature and role of the ministry, but remember, the conversation partners for *BEM* included Catholics with their long history of popes and cardinals and bishops, at the same table with Baptists, whose clergy are ordained by local congregations. The spread was rather wide, and in many ways it is a wonder and a gift of grace that a common statement on ministry could be produced at all.

The Ministry section begins, quite properly, by reminding us that all Christians are ministers. The Holy Spirit calls people to faith and gives them gifts to use in their ministry of witness and service. All members of Christian congregations "are called to discover, with the help of the community, the gifts they have received and to use them for the building up of the Church and for the service of the world to which the Church is sent."[3] In other words, there is no room here for calling the church "Pastor Maynard's church." The church belongs to Christ, and the Holy Spirit empowers all of its members to be ministers.

However, *BEM* goes on to say that the church needs ordained clergy and that they are extremely important to congregational worship and ministry. Why? Because they serve as a kind of focal point for the gifts and energies of the whole community. The church, says *BEM*, needs "persons who are publicly and continually responsible for pointing to its fundamental dependence upon Jesus Christ, and thereby provide, within a multiplicity of gifts, a focus of its unity."[4] This does not mean that ordained ministers are a special class of spiritual beings. They do not stand above everybody else; rather they stand in the middle, at the center of the circle, representing all the spiritual gifts that everyone brings to the church. Ordained ministers are in some ways like the faceted, mirrored globes that revolve in dance halls. They take light from other sources and scatter it around the whole room. So, as *BEM* puts it, the ordained ministry "has no existence apart from the community," and clergy "can fulfill their calling only in and for the community."

How do they do this? What are ordained ministers supposed to do? Simply put, the clergy are to use their gifts and energies to enhance everybody else's. "They serve," states *BEM*, "to build up the community in Christ and to strengthen its witness." Ordained ministers are examples of "holiness and loving concern," and they form "a visible focus of the deep and all-embracing communion between Christ and the members of the body."[5]

Indeed, it is in this way that the leaders of the vital churches could be called strong and charismatic. They are not the grinning television evangelists with the "beautiful people" hairstyles and the Colgate smiles, and they are not the larger-than-life personalities whose congregations gather around them in dependent, cultlike fashion. They are people of deep integrity who have the power to bless others, the willingness to act in Christlike ways as they lead, and the ability to allow a service of worship to be a place of honest hospitality and the sharing of gifts. Of course, like all of us, they are flawed human beings who make mistakes and have selfish desires and sometimes choose the wrong things. But though they sometimes step off the path of obedience, it is walking this path that forms the central theme in their leadership.

STRONG, LOVING, AND WISE

Admittedly, *BEM* was not directly addressing the issue of clergy personality and style in worship, but it nonetheless provides some helpful language and categories for discussing this concern. Here are some insights and implications we can draw, both from BEM and also from the examples of the vital churches:

1. *The worship leader should establish positive personal connection with the congregation.* It is crucial that the leaders of worship establish a positive, personal, and dynamic connection with the congregation. However, as we have noted, this approach is not to be confused with popular notions of charisma, attractiveness, or motivation. The leaders seek to relate to the worshipers as Christ relates to them, or as BEM puts it, represent the "deep and all-embracing communion between Christ and the members of the body." The worship leader expresses kindness and hospitality not to show that the leader is a "nice person" but because this is how Christ greets the community. The worship leader displays enthusiasm, energy, passion, and loving concern not to show that the leader is "dynamic" but because this is how Christ relates to others. The worship leader conducts the service with a quiet inner calm, a nonanxious sense of pace and timing, and reverence not to show that the leader is a "really spiritual" person but because this is honestly how one who belongs to Christ and serves in Christ's name discerns the realities of worship.

Some worship leaders today become confused and try to make their own magnetic personalities the centerpiece of worship. Worship leaders should instead seek to allow the interpersonal dynamics of worship to point always beyond themselves to the relationship between the people and God. Instead of trying to be powerful, popular, and adored, they should seek instead to be "strong, loving, and wise."[6]

The expression of "strong, loving, and wise" worship leadership that I observed in one of the vital churches is not untypical of them all. As worship began, the primary worship leader, the rector of the church, entered with the choir and the other clergy in procession. He was leading the procession, but not with pomp. He walked as the first among equals, turning calmly now and then to look with approval at those following. He moved slowly, but confidently and joyfully, like someone who was leading others to a place of wonder and hope, a place they would like to go. It happened that, on this day, the church was honoring and giving thanks to the firefighters and police in the neighborhood of the church, and representatives of these groups were in the procession, a half-step behind the rector. The rector made it clear by the way he walked with them, sometimes stepping back to touch a shoulder reassuringly or pausing to motion to them gently, that he was already making a place of hospitality and thanksgiving for them in the service. Every now and then he would notice someone in the congregation who perhaps needed a special welcome—a child, a visitor, a person whom he knew to be in special need—and he would step momentarily out of the processional to extend a brief personal greeting—a glance, a touch, or a word. When the procession arrived at the chancel area, the rector did not march single-mindedly to his seat; he was alert to the presence of the others, allowing his eyes and body to anticipate their movements. He acted like a gracious host welcoming guests warmly into his home.

As the rector conducted portions of the service, it was evident that he possessed significant gifts of personality and charm, but these gifts were unwaveringly used to shine the light on others, not on himself. He handled the parish announcements not as a string of notices but as a series of blessings upon those who were serving or teaching or praying. It was evident that he cared about the events and people he mentioned. His prayers were paced with calm and genuine concern, and they named names—the sick, the grieving, those recently married, and those who were new parents. When others were leading the service, he did not sit passively or impatiently, as though he were biding the time waiting for his next turn. He gave his full and responsive attention to their leadership.

In sum, within his human limitations, this worship leader conveyed the very presence of Christ by his manner, his strength, his calm, his attention to others, his spirit of hospitality, and his willingness to serve. His words and actions became, to use the language of *BEM*, a model of "the deep and all-embracing communion between Christ and the members of the body."

2. *The leader should gather the gifts of the congregation.* A number of years ago at Christmastime, Mendelssohn's *Elijah* was performed at Lincoln Center by the New York Philharmonic Orchestra and the Westminster Choir. The evening was a triumph; the orchestra was splendid, the chorus richly resonant, the soloists exciting. Particularly impressive, though, was conductor Kurt Masur. Although he had been called to the podium on only a few weeks' notice because Leonard Bernstein, who was scheduled to conduct that night, had died suddenly, Masur was firmly and confidently prepared. He knew the power of the text; he sensed the promise of the moment, and his body conveyed a joyful excitement over being a part of this event. Masur took gentle command of the musicians, not as a way of flexing his authority but to summon from them their best gifts. When the audience responded to the performance with a standing ovation, Masur beamed toward the singers and the players and then moved his hand over them in an arc of blessing, a benediction. He was in all ways the leader, but his every effort was in support of the others, the music, the event. Ironically, it was his very willingness to lead with such firm compassion and alertness that finally directed the attention away from himself. We did not ultimately have an evening of Kurt Masur; because of Kurt Masur, we had an evening of Mendelssohn.[7]

Kurt Masur sets a powerful example for the leadership of worship. A strong worship leader remains in command, not as a manipulative presence but as one who lovingly expects and summons the very best from the congregation. Such a worship leader recognizes that the Holy Spirit lavishes gifts on the community of faith, and one of the main responsibilities of the leader is to gather these gifts and allow them to be put into service.

For instance, the pastor of one of the vital congregations makes it a point to know what talents and skills the members of her congregation possess. She then makes a place in worship for the exercise of these gifts and orchestrates them so that worship moves with dramatic power. On a given Sunday, one member of the congregation sings a solo accompanied by another on the guitar; another member, an artist, prepares original art on the biblical text for the day, which is displayed in the lobby and adorns the bulletin cover; yet another member, trained in oral performance, reads the scriptural lessons; and still another, a poet, leads the prayers of the people she has helped to compose. In lesser hands, such an amalgam of talent could come across as a variety show, but this worship leader is an "orchestra conductor," not an emcee. She takes the variety of gifts brought to the service, receives them, blesses them, and makes them obedient to the over-all score of worship.

Another vital-church pastor invited a ten-year-old girl to read one of the Scripture lessons. There is nothing unusual about this; children read the Bible in many churches. Often, though, as the child reads, a "gosh-isn't-that-child-cute" feeling washes over the congregation. In this case, though, as the girl stepped up to the lectern, the minister removed the stole from his own shoulders and slowly placed it with great dignity around the shoulders of the child, as if to say, "She is serving as a leader, reading the Word of God."

We return to a point hinted at in chapter 3, namely that the skillful leader of worship knows that two of the most important actions of worship, in the symbolic sense, are receiving the offering and pronouncing the benediction. Every person brings gifts to worship—the gift of prayer, of music and song, of testimony, of discernment, and others. The responsibility of the leader is to receive those gifts, to allow them to be placed on the altar of praise, and to pronounce the blessing of God upon them.

3. *The primary leader should share the leadership of worship with others. BEM* stated that the pastor's authority "is exercised with the coop-eration of the whole community,"[8] and in every case in the vital churches the primary worship leader (usually the rector or senior pastor) shared the leadership of worship with others. Also in every case, this leadership in-cluded women and men, youth and adults. There was never the sense of a quota being met ("OK, a man just spoke; it's now time for a woman"); instead there was a sense of the fullness of a congregation's spiritual gifts and charisms being drawn into the energy of worship. Moreover, one never felt that the worship leaders were "taking turns" ("OK, I'm done; now you're up"), but that they were working together as a team toward a greater goal.

4. *The worship leader should, in word and action, embody the holy character of worship.* In his book *The Church in the Power of the Spirit*, theologian Jürgen Moltmann describes what happens when people step for-ward to lead worship:

[T]he community gathers to hear the proclamation, or for a bap-tism, the common meal, for the feast and to talk together. Then one person or more gets up in front of the congregation in order to preach the Gospel, to baptize, to prepare the meal, to arrange the feast, and to make his contribution to the discussion. These people come from the community but come forward in front of it and act in Christ's name. It is not they as "office bearers" who "confront" the congregation; it is Christ. . . . They come from God's people, stand up in front of God's people and act in God's name.[9]

Notice the dual role of the worship leader as both an ordinary member of the assembly and a representative of Christ. The worship leader comes *from* the gathered body but comes forward and stands *in front of* the assembly to assume a new role: to speak and act in the name of Christ. *BEM* underscores this point when it states that it is "Christ [who] gathers, teaches, and nourishes the Church. It is Christ who invites to the meal and who presides at it. In most churches this presidency is *signified and represented* by an ordained minister."[10]

What happens when worship leaders correctly perceive this dual role? First, there is a sense of freedom. The service of worship does not ultimately depend upon them. It is Christ who is present, Christ who gathers the faithful, Christ who preaches, Christ who teaches and nourishes and intercedes in prayer. In observing worship in the vital churches, I never got from the worship leaders the "hot and bothered" feeling one often gets from worship leaders who fear that the success of worship rises or falls on their efforts. This is not to say that these worship leaders were not as occupied as any others with the details of worship—managing the flow of the service, remembering all the announcements, cueing the musicians, and so on. But there was an inner calm about them, even when they were conveying excitement about the Gospel, a freedom born of the awareness that God is present and active in worship, a this-is-not-finally-about-me attitude that was palpable.

It is said that Angelo Roncalli, better known as Pope John XXIII, would end his day with prayers, and then he would regain a sense of freedom from the crushing weight of his pastoral responsibilities by saying this to himself: "But who governs the church? You or the Holy Spirit? Very well then, go to sleep, Angelo." Just so, effective worship leaders seem to have an inner voice that constantly asks, "Who is really leading these people? You or the Holy Spirit? Very well, then, relax and be free."

Because effective worship leaders possess the freedom that comes from an awareness of God's presence, they also communicate this awareness to the congregation in the way they speak and act. In chapter 2, we talked about the impact of "presidential style," how it is that the way one leads worship reveals the leader's true convictions about what is happening in the sanctuary. If the worship leader honestly believes that God is present here, it shows. Conversely, if the worship leader lacks the awareness of the holy, that too shows.

In the vital churches, the worship leaders handled the symbols and objects of worship—the Bible, the baptismal water, the bread and the wine of the Lord's Supper—with calm reverence. They touched and lifted and carried these objects not superstitiously or with some mechanical pomp and circumstance, but with a combination of loving familiarity and respectful care, as though these objects were treasured gifts of great value.

The leaders in the vital churches also communicated in word and action that the congregation was there to worship. This seems obvious, but it is astonishing how often worship leaders convey to the congregation that there must be some utilitarian reason for their presence. Surely, these leaders imply, the congregation has come primarily to learn or to become better people or to hold their families together or make new friends, anything but worship.

Kennon Callahan notes that this tendency to overlook worship can often be heard in the standard welcome to visitors, which he says goes something like this:

> Those of you who are visiting with us this morning, we want you
> to know how glad we are to have you visiting with us, and we
> hope you will come back and visit with us again when you can.

One of the problems with such a greeting, Callahan notes, is that it suggests that these people are visiting. "They are not simply visiting—they came to worship," he reminds us. "Referring to their coming as a 'visit' indicates that we are trivializing their situation." It is far better, he suggests, to say something like, "Those of you who are worshiping here for the first time, welcome. We are glad we can worship God together this morning."[11]

The leaders of worship in the vital churches spoke in voices that can be described as public, warm, and energetically conversational. First, they spoke in a public voice. Leading worship demands more than a private presence, and it was clear that these leaders were in a public place and speaking to a group. But, second, their voices were also warm; there was none of the shrill tone or the overly dramatic voice of leaders who fear that if they don't infuse this event with some urgency, none will be present. Third, they were energetically conversational. There was electricity in their voices—after all, they were speaking of important things—but the patterns and tones were conversational. They were in the presence of others, who were to be heard and respected. They were not barking orders or shouting at people to shape up; they were leading friends in Christ in worship.

Many years ago, when I was beginning my own ministry, I realized that I was finding the duties of Sunday worship leadership to be an increasing burden. I was spending hours and hours on the sermon, hoping to hit a home run every time. I was fretting about every detail of the service, anxious that each Sunday go flawlessly. I greeted every Sunday with a measure of dread, and, at the end of each service, I felt emotionally and physically spent. At one level, I was being a responsible pastor, eager to ensure that worship was well planned and carried out with excellence. But my anxiety went well beyond good planning and careful execution. It was insecurity born of inexperience and a distorted (even faithless) understanding of how much of the effectiveness of worship depended upon me and my efforts.

At one point, I confided my burdens to an older and wiser pastor, a trusted friend and mentor. He gently reminded me of my mortal status and of the fact that worship finally depends upon God and not the clergy. And then he added, "Long after your sermons are forgotten, your congregation will remember whether you had fun preaching them." It seemed a little flip at the time. Fun preaching sermons? But I think now I understand and appreciate what he was saying. There is a joyfulness at the heart of healthy worship leadership, a deep and abiding cheer that grows out of freedom and faith and is itself a communication of the Gospel.

It is recorded that when the people heard Jesus teach and preach, they listened to him "with delight" (Mark 12:37). Maybe part of the reason this was so was because he spoke "with delight," too.

CHAPTER 10

Epilogue:
Can Revitalized Worship Happen Here?

A cartoon depicts a church cemetery. At the center of the frame is the tombstone of a clergyman. The epitaph reads: "He tried to change the order of worship."

Every church member and every pastor would love for congregational worship to become more vital, more exciting, more faithful to the Gospel, and more appealing to people outside the church. But getting there means real change, and significant change is almost always difficult, threatening, and controversial. The road to renewal in worship is filled with obstacles, sharp turns, and rough stretches of pavement. As we have explored the examples of congregations with vital and faithful worship, many of us have perhaps wondered, "Can our congregation travel that road? Can we change in regard to worship? Can the marks of the vital and faithful congregations become a part of our own church's worship life? Can it happen here?"

FOUR INSIGHTS

While no words of advice can completely smooth and straighten the way, the lessons of the vital and faithful congregations can be instructive. When we consider how it is that change happened in these churches, four insights about congregational worship reform can be identified:

1. *Pastoral leadership is the key to worship renewal.* The main responsibility for worship renewal rests firmly on the shoulders of the pastoral leadership of a church. I suppose it would be neater, cleaner, and theologically sweeter to claim that the impulse and wisdom for worship

reform rises up from the whole body of the church, but the practical reality is that if the pastor doesn't move it, worship doesn't move. Even when the hunger for something new and more nourishing in worship wells up from the congregation, it is the pastor who almost always must provide the impetus, shape, and direction of change.

Indeed, in all of the vital congregations, the renewal of worship happened because the pastor of the church had a vision of what worship could be and boldly took steps to put that vision into practice. Sometimes this meant simply making changes unilaterally, seeking forgiveness instead of permission; in other cases, the changes were done more collegially and with higher regard for normal congregational process. But in every situation, the pastor took a strong and leading role, calling upon skills of persuasion and diplomacy and depending upon the force of personality to bring the congregation along.

2. *Whenever worship is renewed, some congregational conflict is inevitable.* Obviously, then, we are in dangerous territory when we enter the realm of worship change. Change is volatile and controversial, much depends upon the pastor, and therefore, pastors who are unwise or unhealthy can generate serious congregational conflict or lead congregations astray and severely damage the worship and missional life of the church.

The line is thin here between strong leadership and strong-arm leadership. It is one thing when a caring and discerning pastor, one who has a healthy relationship with the congregation and a keen and theologically rich understanding of worship, firmly leads a church to a new and vital place in worship that the members do not yet comprehend and where they would not otherwise be ready to go. It is quite another thing for a pastor to be motivated by arrogance, to have an "I have better taste than they do" attitude about worship, and as a result to force the congregation to swallow some liturgical castor oil because it is good for them.

I think it was Justice Oliver Wendell Holmes who once said, "Even a dog knows the difference between being tripped over and being kicked." Just so, congregations know when they are being stretched and challenged to worship more effectively and when they are being bullied into submission by a leader with a chip on the shoulder. Even so, the healthiest of worship reforms encouraged by the gentlest and wisest of pastors will always be accompanied by some measure of conflict. There will be complaints; some people may stay away from worship, even leave the church. We should hope this will not happen, but not to be prepared for it is to be foolishly naïve about the power and threat of worship change.

3. *To change worship, significant lay involvement is necessary.* Even though the initiative for worship change lies primarily with the pastoral staff, clergy alone cannot and should not carry the full weight of worship reform. Key leaders in the congregation ought to be brought on board early. The pastor needs to articulate the vision clearly and firmly, but a wise pastor will also seek and respect the counsel of lay leaders. If there isn't a strong worship committee already in place, one should be formed, and it should be guided toward a mission of education, planning, and monitoring of congregational response to worship changes. If an already extant worship committee is moribund, it should be reshuffled and revived. Some feathers may be ruffled, but nothing is more urgent to congregational health and faithfulness than effective worship.

Also, as we have already seen in previous chapters, real worship reform involves an increase in congregational participation in worship. The pastoral leadership should irrigate the fields of worship with the refreshing waters flowing from the worshipers. Pastors would do well to open up the church directory and go down the list name by name, asking, "What skill, talent, or charism does this person bring to worship, and how can it be effectively used?" Once these are identified, these people should be invited to exercise their gifts in worship.

4. *Education and publicity help pave the way for worship renewal.* Whenever a congregation enters a season of worship renewal, a program of education about worship and about the purpose and meaning of the changes should be established. Articles in the church newsletter, courses in the church school curriculum, information and talk-back sessions, book studies, moments for teaching set in the context of worship, sermons, letters, e-mail announcements, and brochures are among the means that can be employed.

These educational efforts should include both children and adults. They should be aimed at the faithful and regular "insiders" and at those who rarely attend and who would see themselves as on the margins of the church's life. Some people will take advantage of these opportunities and will become more educated about the theology and character of worship. Others will treat these efforts as merely publicity and data sharing.

Regardless of the level of involvement, though, everyone will be given a signal that worship is urgent and that worship is ever being renewed. Moreover, they will be provided with some common vocabulary to speak of the changes, and no one will be blindsided when the atmosphere in the worship space becomes electric with energy and excitement.

The cartoon tombstone inscription "He tried to change the order of worship" is amusing. A far sadder epitaph would be, "This person saw a vision of what vibrant and effective worship could be but decided to do nothing about it."

May God richly bless you as you seek to enable your congregation to worship more faithfully and to find itself "lost in wonder, love, and praise."

Preface

1. Annie Dillard, *Teaching a Stone to Talk* (New York: HarperCollins, 1982), 58.
2. Ibid, 58.
3. Fleming Rutledge, *Help My Unbelief* (Grand Rapids: Eerdmans, 2000), 193.
4. From the Charles Wesley hymn "Love Divine, All Loves Excelling."

Chapter 1

1. See Donald Miller, *Reinventing American Protestantism: Christianity in the New Millennium* (Berkeley: University of California Press, 1997).
2. James F. White, *Christian Worship in North America: A Retrospective: 1955-1995* (Collegeville, Minn.: Liturgical Press, 1997), 33-43.
3. The names Harry and Mary Seeker come from Lee Strobel, *Inside the Mind of Unchurched Harry and Mary* (Grand Rapids: Zondervan, 1993). Strobel is a leader at the Willow Creek Community Church in suburban Chicago.
4. Bill Hybels, "Willow Creek Community Church," in *The New Apostolic Churches*, edited by C. Peter Wagner (Ventura, Calif.: Regal, 1998), 80.
5. Ibid, 80.
6. Texas businessman and author Bob Buford as quoted in Charles Trueheart, "Welcome to the Next Church," *The Atlantic Monthly*, 278/2 (Aug. 1996). The article can also be found on the Internet at www.theatlantic.com/issues/96aug/nxtchrch/nxtchrch.html, and it is from the Web version that this quotation is taken (p. 10).
7. C. Peter Wagner, "The New Apostolic Reformation" in *The New Apostolic Churches*, 22.
8. Sally Morgenthaler, *Worship Evangelism: Inviting Unbelievers into the Presence of God* (Grand Rapids: Zondervan, 1999) 44-45.
9. A preacher at the Vineyard Church "Catch the Fire Service," as quoted in Jackson W. Carroll, *Mainline to the Future: Congregations for the 21st Century* (Louisville: Westminster John Knox, 2000), 54.

10. See Robert E. Webber, *Blended Worship: Achieving Substance and Relevance in Worship* (Peabody, Mass.: Hendrickson, 1996), and *Planning Blended Worship: The Creative Mixture of Old and New* (Nashville: Abingdon, 1998).

Chapter 2

1. Robert N. Bellah, et al., *Habits of the Heart: Individualism and Commitment in American Life* (Berkeley: University of California Press, 1985), 228.

2. Marva J. Dawn, *A Royal "Waste" of Time: The Splendor of Worshiping God and Being Church for the World* (Grand Rapids: Eerdmans, 1999).

3. *The Heidelberg Catechism* (Cleveland: United Church Press, 1962).

4. Ernst Becker, *The Denial of Death* (New York: Free Press, 1973), 285.

5. Barbara Brown Taylor, *The Preaching Life* (Cambridge and Boston: Cowley Publications, 1993), 47.

6. Frederick Buechner, *Telling the Truth: The Gospel as Tragedy, Comedy, and Fairy Tale* (New York: Harper & Row, 1977), 40.

7. Robert W. Hovda, *Strong, Loving, and Wise: Presiding in Liturgy* (Washington: Liturgical Conference, 1976), 75.

8. Gordon W. Lathrop, *Holy Things: A Liturgical Theology* (Minneapolis: Fortress, 1993), chapter 5, especially 119-127.

9. James E. Dittes, *The Church in the Way* (New York: Scribner's, 1967), 332-339.

10. Frederick Buechner, *The Magnificent Defeat* (New York: Seabury, 1966), 79-80.

Chapter 3

1. Curiously, door-to-door and telephone surveys of Americans indicate that worship attendance has remained remarkably stable over the last half-century. The problem is that the huge number of people who "remember" attending church in the last seven days does not square up with actual counts of people in the pews. As one analyst put it, "Americans are—to put it delicately—prone to optimism when they answer sociologists' questions about church attendance." Some researchers think that the overreporting may be as high as 50 percent. See Alan Ryan, "My Way," *New York Review of Books*, XLVII/13 (Aug. 10, 2000), 47-50.

2. Robert Putnam, *Bowling Alone: The Collapse and Revival of American Community* (New York: Simon & Schuster, 2000).

3. Trueheart, "Welcome to the Next Church" (Internet version), 1.

4. Timothy Wright, *A Community of Joy: How to Create Contemporary Worship*, Herb Miller, ed. (Nashville: Abingdon, 1994), 20-21.

5. Ibid., 37.

6. Ibid., 38-49.

7. Trueheart, "Welcome to the Next Church" (Internet version), 15.

8. Morgenthaler, *Worship Evangelism*, 78.

9. Ibid., 77-78.

10. Richard Sennett, *The Fall of Public Man: On the Social Psychology of Capitalism* (New York: Random House, 1978), 257ff. See the excellent treatment of Sennett in Patrick R. Keifert, *Welcoming the Stranger: A Public Theology of Worship and Evangelism* (Minneapolis: Fortress, 1992), 16-26.

11. Tim and Cathy Carson, *So You're Thinking About Contemporary Worship* (St. Louis: Chalice, 1997), 31-32, emphasis in the original.

12. Hendrikus Berkhof, *Christian Faith: An Introduction to the Study of the Faith* (Grand Rapids: Eerdmans, 1979), 17.

13. Parker Palmer, *The Company of Strangers* (New York: Crossroad, 1981), 17-35.

14. Keifert, *Welcoming the Stranger*, 80.

15. Christine D. Pohl, *Making Room: Recovering Hospitality as a Christian Tradition* (Grand Rapids: Eerdmans, 1999), 172.

16. *Didiscalia et Constitutiones Apostolorum* 2.58.6, edited by F. X. Funk (Paderborn: Scheoningh, 1905), vol. 1, 168, as quoted in Gordon W. Lathrop, *Holy Things*, 120.

17. Lathrop, *Holy Things*, 121.

18. Brother Jeremiah, quoted in Alan Jones, *Soul Making: The Desert Way of Spirituality* (San Francisco: HarperSanFrancicso, 1985), 13.

19. Robert Hovda, *The Amen Corner*, John F. Baldovin, ed. (Collegeville, Minn.: Pueblo, 1994), 140.

20. Ibid., 140.

21. Kennon L. Callahan, *Dynamic Worship: Mission, Grace, Praise, and Power* (San Francisco: Jossey-Bass, 1994), 16.

22. Ibid., 11-15.

23. Ibid., 15.

Chapter 4

1. William Sloane Coffin, Jr., "Our Resurrection, Too," in *The Riverside Preachers*, Paul H. Sherry, ed. (New York: Pilgrim, 1978), 162.

2. Marva Dawn, *Reaching Out Without Dumbing Down: A Theology of Worship for the Turn-of-the-Century Culture* (Grand Rapids: Eerdmans, 1995), 123.

3. Robert E. Webber, *Worship Is a Verb* (Dallas: Word, 1985), 29.

4. Tex Sample, *The Spectacle of Worship in a Wired World: Electronic Culture and the Gathered People of God* (Nashville: Abingdon, 1998), 107.

5. Webber, *Worship Is a Verb*, 38.

6. Dillard, *Teaching a Stone to Talk*, 38.

Chapter 5

1. Michael S. Hamilton, "The Triumph of the Praise Songs: How Guitars Beat Out the Organ in the Worship Wars," *Christianity Today*, 43/8 (July 12, 1999), 30.

2. Sample, *The Spectacle of Worship in a Wired World*, 36.

3. Ibid., 36.

4. Tex Sample, *Ministry in an Oral Culture*, 78-79.

5. Brian Wren, *Praying Twice: The Music and Words of Congregational Song* (Louisville: Westminster John Knox, 2000), 197.

6. Ibid., 205.

7. Ibid., 217.

8. Thomas Day, *Why Catholics Can't Sing: The Culture of Catholicism and the Triumph of Bad Taste* (New York: Crossroad, 1990), 64.

9. Ibid., 60.

10. Brian Wren, copyright © 1998, Praise Partners Publications. All rights reserved. Used by permission. As quoted in Wren, *Praying Twice*, 225.

11. Day, *Why Catholics Can't Sing*, 62.

12. See also Martin Tel's excellent discussion of the interplay between "excellence" and "relevance" in church music in "Music: The 'Universal Language' That's Dividing the Church," in *Making Room at the Table: An Invitation to Multicultural Worship*, Brian K. Blount and Leonora Tubbs Tisdale, eds. (Louisville: Westminster John Knox, 2001), 162-174.

Chapter 6

1. James F. White and Susan J. White, *Church Architecture: Building and Renovating for Christian Worship* (Nashville: Abingdon, 1988), 11.

2. Throughout this chapter, as I have done in other places in this book, I use the word "sanctuary" in its most popular sense, namely, to refer to the whole room where worship takes place. In more formal discussions of the liturgy and church architecture, "sanctuary" is sometimes used in its more precise sense to describe the section of a worship building reserved to the clergy.

3. White and White, *Church Architecture*, 16.

4. Ibid., 16.

5. See William Willimon, *Word, Water, Wine, and Bread: How Worship Has Changed Over the Years* (Valley Forge: Judson, 1980), 9-19.

6. White and White, *Church Architecture*, 18. Actually, instead of naming seven spaces, the authors name six "spaces" and three "liturgical centers." It is far from clear, though, how they are distinguishing a "space" from a "liturgical center," especially since two of the "liturgical centers," altar-table and baptismal font or pool, are also listed as "spaces." When we add the six "spaces" to the one remaining "liturgical center" not named as a "space" (the pulpit-lectern), we get seven distinct areas of worship action.

7. Ibid., 10-11.

Chapter 8

1. C. S. Lewis, *Letters to Malcolm: Chiefly on Prayer* (New York: Harcourt, Brace, & World, 1963), 4.

2. This prayer, which is in the public domain, can be found in *The Oxford Book of Prayer* (Oxford, England: Oxford University Press, 1985), 75.

3. Walter J. Ong, *Orality and Literacy: The Technologizing of the Word* (New York: Methuen, 1982), 74.

4. Webber, *Planning Blended Worship*, 20-21.

5. Ibid., 21.

6. Henry H. Mitchell, *Celebration and Experience in Preaching* (Nashville: Abingdon, 1990), 66.

Chapter 9

1. Callahan, *Dynamic Worship*, 22.

2. *Baptism, Eucharist, and Ministry: Faith and Order Paper No. 111* (Geneva, Switzerland: World Council of Churches, 1982).

3. Ibid., Ministry Section, para. 5.

4. Ibid., Ministry Section, para. 8.

5. Ibid., Ministry Section, paras. 12 and 14.

6. These words, from a translation of 2 Timothy 1:6-7, are used by liturgical scholar Robert Hovda as the title of his book on worship leadership: *Strong, Loving, and Wise: Presiding in Liturgy* (Washington: The Liturgical Conference, 1977). The full translation of the text is as follows: "I remind you to stir into flame the gift of God bestowed when my hands were laid upon you. The Spirit God has given us is no cowardly spirit, but rather one that makes us strong, loving, and wise."

7. See my description of this event in "Liturgical Storm Clouds," *Theology Today*, XLVIII/1 (April 1991), 4.

8. *BEM*, Ministry Section, para. 15.

9. Jürgen Moltmann, *The Church in the Power of the Spirit: A Contribution to Messianic Ecclesiology* (New York: Harper & Row, 1977), 303.

10. *BEM*, Ministry Section, para. 14, emphasis added.

11. Callahan, *Dynamic Worship*, 23-24.

Authentic Worship in a Changing Culture. Grand Rapids: CRC Publications, 1997. Produced as a study document by the Christian Reformed Church, this little booklet on changing trends in worship has a refreshingly sound grasp on how to keep worship true to the Gospel but also open to change. A concluding section of questions and answers on nuts-and-bolts topics, such as announcements, minidramas, and woeful choirs, is particularly helpful.

Baptism, Eucharist, and Ministry: Faith and Order Paper No. 111. Geneva, Switzerland: World Council of Churches, 1982. A significant document of the World Council of Churches, expressing a theological convergence of the ecumenical church on the critical issues of baptism, eucharist, and the forms and orders of ministry.

Callahan, Kennon L. *Dynamic Worship: Mission, Grace, Praise, and Power.* San Francisco: Jossey-Bass, 1994. In this very practical book, the author of *Twelve Keys to an Effective Church* turns his attention to worship. He emphasizes infusing worship with hospitality and excitement to make worship attractive to newcomers.

Carroll, Jackson. *Mainline to the Future: Congregations for the 21st Century.* Louisville: Westminster John Knox, 2000. A solid and thoughtful discussion of the plight of the old "mainline" churches and a vision for the renewal of congregations, including a brief consideration of worship.

Dawn, Marva J. *Reaching Out Without Dumbing Down: A Theology of Worship for the Turn-of-the-Century Culture.* Grand Rapids: Eerdmans, 1995; and *A Royal "Waste" of Time: The Splendor of Worshiping God and Being Church for the World.* Grand Rapids: Eerdmans, 1999. The first book is a major contribution to the literature of worship reform, a strong, well-written, and carefully argued call for theological substance in worship. The second book is a splendid collection of essays and sermons on the same theme.

Day, Thomas. *Why Catholics Can't Sing: The Culture of Catholicism and the Triumph of Bad Taste.* New York: Crossroad, 1990. A hilarious complaint about the agonies of church music, Catholic or otherwise.

Hamilton, Michael S. "The Triumph of the Praise Songs: How Guitars Beat Out the Organ in the Worship Wars," *Christianity Today*, vol. 43, no. 8, July 12, 1999), 28ff. (also available on the Internet at www.christianitytoday.com/ct/9t8/9ts8028.html). A professor of history at Notre Dame provides a keen and open-minded discussion of musical styles in worship.

Hovda, Robert W. *Strong, Loving, and Wise: Presiding in Liturgy.* Washington: Liturgical Conference, 1976. Written primarily for Roman Catholic priests but applicable ecumenically, this book focuses on the task of leading worship. Hovda gives practical suggestions for how worship presiders can embody the Gospel in the way worship is conducted.

Keifert, Patrick R. *Welcoming the Stranger: A Public Theology of Worship and Evangelism.* Minneapolis: Fortress, 1992. Keifert argues that, in many churches, psychological notions of intimacy and friendship have replaced the biblical concept of hospitality to the stranger, and he points the way toward reclaiming the biblical idea of welcoming strangers in the name of Christ.

Miller, Donald. *Reinventing American Protestantism: Christianity in the New Millennium.* Berkeley: University of California Press, 1997. In an often-cited discussion of the shifts in North American church life, Miller gives special attention to the "new paradigm" churches, those that have significantly departed from traditional forms of church structure, worship, and evangelism.

Morgenthaler, Sally. *Worship Evangelism: Inviting Unbelievers into the Presence of God.* Grand Rapids: Zondervan, 1999. Writing from an evangelical theological perspective, Morgenthaler is appreciative but finally critical of many of the methods of "seeker-friendly" worship. She advocates moving from a "what works" approach to a more theologically grounded worship reform.

Pohl, Christine D. *Making Room: Recovering Hospitality as a Christian Tradition.* Grand Rapids: Eerdmans, 1999. A brilliant treatment of the Christian practice of hospitality, including hospitality in worship. Pohl treats history, theology, and practical matters.

Putnam, Robert. *Bowling Alone: The Collapse and Revival of American Community.* New York: Simon & Schuster, 2000. In one of the most talked-about books of the last decade, Putnam laments the decline in social capital, the glue that holds together society's institutions, including the church, and recommends ways to restore confidence and commitment.

Sample, Tex. *The Spectacle of Worship in a Wired World: Electronic Culture and the Gathered People of God.* Nashville: Abingdon, 1998. A provocative and witty account of how worship needs to change in a "wired," cyber-tuned world.

Senn, Frank C. *New Creation: A Liturgical Worldview.* Minneapolis: Fortress, 2000. A nuanced and theologically sophisticated treatment of contemporary issues facing the church's worship by the noted Lutheran liturgical scholar. His emphasis falls most firmly on the traditional side.

Trueheart, Charles, "Welcome to the Next Church," *The Atlantic Monthly*, vol. 278, no. 2, Aug. 1996 (also can be found on the Internet at www.theatlantic.com/issues/96aug/nxtchrch/nxtchrch.htm. A fascinating journalistic account of the Willow Creek–style churches, their methods and goals. Contains quotations from many of the new-paradigm church pastors and leaders.

Webber, Robert E., *Blended Worship: Achieving Substance and Relevance in Worship*. Peabody, Mass.: Hendrickson, 1996; and *Planning Blended Worship: The Creative Mixture of Old and New*. Nashville: Abingdon, 1998. Creative proposals for blending traditional and contemporary forms of worship. Leans toward the traditional in terms of worship structure, and the contemporary in terms of worship language and music.

White, James F., *Christian Worship in North America: A Retrospective: 1955-1995*. Collegeville, Minn.: Liturgical Press, 1997. A clear, concise, and readable treatment of recent developments in worship in North America from a leading liturgical scholar.

White, James F., and Susan J. White. *Church Architecture: Building and Renovating for Christian Worship*. Nashville: Abingdon, 1988. The best available book on church architecture addressed to nonspecialists.

Willimon, William. *Word, Water, Wine, and Bread: How Worship Has Changed Over the Years*. Valley Forge: Judson, 1980. A brief and accessible treatment of the sweep of the history of Christian worship.

Wren, Brian. *Praying Twice: The Music and Words of Congregational Song*. Louisville: Westminster John Knox, 2000. A comprehensive treatment of all aspects of hymnody and congregational song by the well-known hymn writer.

Wright, Timothy. *A Community of Joy: How to Create Contemporary Worship*, Herb Miller, ed. Nashville: Abingdon, 1994. Practical suggestions for creating contemporary, "visitor-friendly" worship from one of the pastors of the Community Church of Joy in Phoenix.